"We wear the masks that grins and lies Hides our cheeks and shades our eyes."

Paul Lawrence Dunbar, Poet

AMERICAN ROBOT

A CULTURAL CHAMELEON RISES ABOVE RACE & RELIGIOUS TRAUMAS

I0626991

AARON ANTHONY VESSUP

Copyright © 2025 by Aaron Anthony Vessup

ISBN: 979-8-88615-326-2 (Paperback)
        979-8-88615-325-5 (Hardback)
        979-8-88615-327-9 (Ebook)

All rights reserved. No part of this publication may be reproduced, distributed, or transmitted in any form or by any means, including photocopying, recording, or other electronic or mechanical methods, without the prior written permission of the publisher, except in the case brief quotations embodied in critical reviews and other noncommercial uses permitted by copyright law.

The views expressed in this book are solely those of the author and do not necessarily reflect the views of the publisher, and the publisher hereby disclaims any responsibility for them.

Inks and Bindings
888-290-5218
www.inksandbindings.com
orders@inksandbindings.com

CONTENTS

CHAPTER 1

BREAKING RULES

1977] I knew I was out of place, but it was already too late. I felt like I'd been caught with my pants down. I was vulnerable. Anything could happen. Coming back into the United States, my wife, Pam, and I were in a tough situation. After a month-long camping trip in Manitoba, Canada, and now hours of driving, our minds were unfocused, and we were a little flaky. We almost forgot that as an interracial couple, we stood out. Pam is a five-foot, ten-inch blonde, who hails from West Virginia and has short hair, light grey eyes, and pale skin that easily burns in the sun. We are equal in height, and as a native Californian, I hope that my easy-going smile, reflects friendliness. I hope that my average height and medium chocolate skin can reflect friendliness. We're both in our late twenties and have gotten used to being subjected to strange, prolonged stares. Heavy, ominous rain clouds made the evening grow dark early. The fact that we hadn't seen gas stations for miles hadn't seemed important before. But now, the fuel tank indicator was stuck in the red zone. We had lost our bet on seeing a gas station soon. Our map was out of date.

Crossing the border between Canada and USA had been a joyful occasion. But now, those feelings of homecoming were long forgotten. My eyes and body were now full alert, my frazzled nerves on edge. In this dark, unfamiliar territory we both felt uneasy. A black man alone with a white woman on a lonely country road is never a good thing. Especially at night. Pam and I enjoyed being together, but we were wise enough to know that not everyone understood that, and sometimes, it caused them to react unpredictably.

We were lost somewhere in northern Pennsylvania. The *Poconos* Mountains could either be close or far away. But even this known landmark didn't matter now. We were in the middle of nowhere. All that kept us going was thoughts of home, a hot shower, and a soft, warm bed.

Suddenly, a strange sound coming from our car engine made my skin tingle and body hairs stand on end. I glanced at my wife whose panicked look mirrored the sinking feeling in my heart. A heavy feeling of panic weighed in the pit of my stomach. Without looking at the dimly lit dashboard I knew the sound meant our gamble had not paid off. We were out of gas. We had been off the interstate cruising a strange dark neighborhood for hours, and now hopes of finding the welcome lights of civilization and gasoline were dashed. Our luck had run out. The unfamiliarity of the area and the silence all around us was killing me.

"Oh shit! You know what this means? That sound?" "Yes. Goddamn it! This isn't good."

"Yep. And the bad news is we don't have a gas can!"

As an interracial couple, a bold symbol of rule breakers, some would say we deserved any misadventure that befell us. And now, here in a dark unknown part of the United States, our new Ford *Pinto,* the ultimate gas-saving automobile, was uttering its final gasps, putting us squarely in the middle of a potential misadventure.

Our anxiety was quickly mounting, and we needed to find assistance soon. This emergency demanded quick thinking. Although we weren't in the American South, which brought some comfort, there was still plenty of cause for worry. Uneasy thoughts crept into my mind. I suddenly recalled the ill-fate of a Chinese student who had been fatally shot simply for knocking on a private residence's door. He had been looking for help in an unwelcoming neighborhood. Now, I would be a black man in an area that reeked of wealth and prosperity. A nail sticking out on a white American chessboard. Pam sat alone in our Ford Pinto. We both thought it would be safer for her to wait while I played the brave adventurer.

Approaching the first home, I noticed that lights were on in several rooms. Slivers of light streaked between thick draperies in the main living room. An ornate shaded lamp with apron fringes sat close to a large window. As I approached the front door, the draperies rustled and then were drawn closed. As I rang the door chimes, and a shadowy figure moved from the window. I knocked on the door and rang the chimes again.

"Hello! Hello! Anybody home? Hello! We need help our car has run out of gas. Hello?"

No answer. Waiting several seconds, I decided not to press my luck. Retreating up the long driveway, I tried the next house. It, too, dimly lit, and again, I knocked and rang the doorbell. Still no luck. The rest of the homes in the area were totally dark.

Walking back to the main road, I saw a Jeep pull into a dark driveway a few houses down. As the vehicle approached the house, property lights automatically illuminated the area. I quickly, I hurried over as a white male stepped out of the Jeep. When I arrived, the wide garage door was slowly closing. Only his legs were visible. My shouts immediately got his attention, and the garage door jerked to a halt and reversed its course.

"Good evening sir! We need help! We've run out of gas. Is there a station nearby? We're returning from a camping trip and are lost," I said as politely and earnestly as I could.

"Sure. There's a station over in that direction," he said pointing. "East. But I can do better than that." He walked over to the side of his garage and started rummaging through the supplies on a shelf. A moment later, he came back over with a gas can. "Here's a gas can with fuel for my lawn mower. It should be enough to get you to the station. Just promise to leave the can there so I can pick it up later, okay?"

"Thank you so-ooo much! I'll be sure to leave the can there. Here are a few dollars for your trouble," I said, reaching for my wallet.

"Nah, forget about it. It's my pleasure to help. Just pay it forward," he said with a smile.

Pam and I were ecstatic. This had been a close call. We knew we were lucky to have this adventure end positively. When we finally got home, it had never looked or felt so good.

Emergencies frequently called for mental jumping jacks, especially for minorities in America. Most black Americans are familiar with having to react to overt or covert hostility.

Unfortunately, the negative outcomes of these encounters often devalue their humanity. I generally try to ignore the automatic bull's eye trained on my back- as it is routinely trained on the back every black man- but the target becomes larger when I am with a white woman.

A mixed couple entering any kind of social situation is automatically taking a risk. They don't know if their mere presence will represent a violation of some personal social code. Not every American has stood for cultural unity.

In the case of my own black family, we were quite divided on the matter of race mixing, despite a staunch espousal of Christian values. My dream of being a cultural ambassador was an important motive long before entering this marriage. It was not my first marriage, and there would be others. There would be other marriages. I am a certified rule-breaker. A social "trouble-maker". This is not intentional. I simply always marched to my own drumbeat.

Having a multifaceted grasp of communications- in all its forms- is essential in such situations. I have several degrees in Speech Communications and have accumulated countless cross-cultural experiences from both work and travel. I wanted to fly high.

CHAPTER 2

ROLE MODELS

E arly one special day, a new reality from the real world was forced upon me. I was shaken to the core.

"Get outta of here nigger!"

That quiet, balmy, sunny morning was abruptly broken by a coarse voice shouting. I had been lost in my own mind bliss, wandering through the thick grass of Inglewood High School. That year of 1953 became etched deep in my total being. The lonely football field gridiron. Dodging the spray of automatic sprinklers. I was conscious of everything within my own mental space. But the loud voice jars me awake.

"Get outta of here nigger!"

A large, beefy, white man whose thick pink neck seemed to have been stuffed between huge shoulder mounds. He charged toward me menacingly, and I suddenly realized that his words were directed at me. My body froze, and water from two circulating sprinklers pummeled me, drenching my shirt and legs.

"Hey you! What are you doing here? Get outta here nigger! Hey! I'm talking to you!" The loud man came closer. Bigger. His stride faster. As he closed in about ten yards away, I saw his red face bulging, neck choking with anger. One large fist raised waving in a threatening gesture. I awoke from my temporary trance, turned and ran in terror. I feared this large monster would catch me. I could barely breathe. Death seemed eminent. My small legs churned too slow on the wet grass, feet slipping barely getting traction. I felt like a mechanical robot having no success running for my life. Then there was a fence and street. I prayed: Get away. Get away. I told myself that I must survive. I must find a circuitous route to reach my father. I ran further away from the grassy football field. My direction was away from *Inglewood High School* where my father is completing an electrical emergency project. That weekend no students or administrators were at the school except my dad and myself. No one, apparently, except the white Custodian, or Coach, who chased me.

Finally, feeling safe I slowly worked my way up and down various back streets. I looked back over my shoulders several times before reaching the front of the school. Then I scooted under the tall chain linked fence at last reaching the annex bungalows. My father was still concentrating on his work. He looked up as I opened and closed the door. I checked to make sure I had not been followed. I still gasped for air as my chest heaved in violent jerks. My shortness of breath caused my father to stare. His eyes narrowed as he spoke.

"Ah, there you are. What's the matter? What happened to you?"

He scrutinized my tear streaked face. My uncontrollable jerky hiccups and short breathing brought a serious look on his face. I had trouble getting coherent words out. Choking with fear and physical exhaustion, my chest and heart both were about to explode. While I felt safe with my father, I still was on the verge of dying. There was no air. No air. No air. I slid down back against the wall, my buttocks hit the cold floor. My eyes closed while my father came closer assessing my tear face and soggy wet clothes. Alarmed, he completely stopped working and interrogated me.

"What happened? Tell me! What happened to you?"

"Tha.. tha... that ma..m-m-m man..." I could barely get my words out.

"Why are you crying? Did someone hit you?" I heard a fierce sound in his voice, intensity flashed from his eyes, and face sterner. I was still in a trace, stuck in the past moment of horror. I had never seen eyes of hate until being chased by the strange White man. Now, I was more terrorized fearing for my life. My dad finally dragged a bit of coherence out of me. He realized something bad had occurred. He left the bungalow after saying, *stay put here.* He returned much later at what seemed to be an eternity. There was a look of satisfaction on his face. I was relived hearing his comforting words.

"It's okay dear. You don't have to worry about that happening again. Some people are just ignorant. They really need Jesus. All we can do is pray."

I did not return to that school with my dad.

I was only seven years old. I had never seen a White person like that. However, there also had been a smiling White nurse in a hospital months earlier. My mother had taken me for flu prevention care. A strange nurse posed in front of me with a terrifying long needle. She seemed happy squirting a stream of liquid in the air. My mother insisted that I lower my pants. The White nurse suddenly hit my buttocks hard administering a Booster shot as if I was an animal. The hypodermic syringe broke. Half of the steel needle was left protruding from my butt. This was the beginning of my fearing Whites. Physical and mental pain.

I could not have foreseen, at that time, that I would ever become friendly with White people. And marriage to a person of that color was the farthest thing from my mind. Ignorance on why Whites hated blacks made me more curious about the invisible wall. From that day on I wanted answers. I was curious. My parents had simple answers like: "You're too young to worry about such things. You'll find out soon enough." This was dad, then terminating the topic with "Just pray for them. They need Jesus." Mother's answer was simpler: "Consider the source. It's ignorance." A few years older I read the story of *Robin Hood.* This tale delighted my imagination. Perhaps I could become some sort of avenging peace maker. I had no idea how, but I assumed from later readings, that Robin Hood was a good hero choice. He used his skills strategically. I reread tales of the Merry men of England's Sherwood Forest over at least five times. *Robin Hood* was an exciting risk-taker. He championed the underdog class.

I Looked at the Black men that frequented our world. They were mostly church folk. I tried to imagine them as brave firemen, or demanding respect from police. But the only ones who seemed manly and potentially brave were the brawny carpenters, plasterers, plumbers, and my dad the electrician. Unfortunately, the only real heroes were men with guns on television. That they were always white perplexed me. Rooting for Tonto's, the sidekick of T.V.s *Lone Ranger* cowboy, was my only consolation. I was also determined to be my father's loyal bible soldier warrior. Everyone assumed this my destiny.

CHAPTER 3

STANDING AMONG MEN

"Your father must be a bully. I don't see how your mother can stay with such a man."

One junior high teacher noticed fresh welts on my back during playground recess. I thought it unfair to say this. My immediate need to defend him was automatic. "Oh...no! My dad is very kind to my mother. He never raises his voice to her. Sometimes he brings her a big box of chocolate *See's Candy*. My dad says that god is love." I did not reveal the word games we played at home…

These words silenced the accuser, but I had missed her point. I failed to realize that anyone could guess the reason why the cloth of my shirt and pants sometimes stuck to my body with dried blood. I still assumed that the aftermath of my weekend punishment I assumed was well hidden. I was smart enough to avoid changing my clothes for gym on the days immediately following a terrible whipping by either pretending to feel sick or finding an excuse to visit the library or principal's office.

In public, my father had a warm smile and a winning personality that made him a popular figure in our community. In private, however, the first five of fifteen children he eventually sired rarely saw this smile. As the second child, in this army of crusading "holy roller" social misfits, I mostly remember my father changing depending on the time, place, and circumstance. I felt proudest to call him my dad when watching him in the music section of our large church, standing among the men when the four-piece brass section rose in unison to play. His small trumpet in his huge hands, shiny, golden, gleaming trumpet looked even smaller in his huge hands. The silver mouthpiece was pressed against his now-serious lips- set within a face marked by concentration. The glorious music made me tingle and my feet twitched. Sometimes I danced in the church aisles. Afterwards I was not whipped for misbehavior.

My father was a handsome black man of six-foot-two-inches. He had broad shoulders, oak-tree legs, gravel-tough hands, and black hair slicked back with sweet-smelling *Murray's* hair grease. In church his 220 pounds were draped in a light-gray pin-striped suit. He looked dapper, talented, and highly respected. No white people attended the large congregation.

When the church music reached its' highest emotional climax, the captivated human throng would ride the waves of cathartic exuberance. Adults would unashamedly jump around, sway, cry out loud and moan. In those moments, I would gaze at my father with pride. He was not yet in heaven, but his name was as hallowed in our home as if he were. I loved to watch him as the magical musician, the undisputed source of the crowd's joy. Dad was not a bad man. Dad a bully was impossible. But he had effective means of training and molding his family. He also was a master robot builder.

At church, he was the perfect image of a doting and beloved father. At home, when his work truck purred into the driveway, and the engine cut-off, we would all chorus in impromptu harmony from various stations around the house, *"Daa-ddyyyy's Ho-mmme!"*

When I was younger and his smiles were not so rare my father's melodious voice and footsteps were happily welcomed. In those days, we were considered a well-off, middle-income family with a certain level of respectability in the neighborhood. But soon things would change: our neighborhood, our station in life, and even our 's image and place in the community.

*****

Young boys fight about many trivial things. One sure way to guarantee a fight, was responding to wise cracks about a persons' family. Our mother attempted to prevent us to avoid fighting by teaching us an old litany. In those early days, mom was patient.

"Just say it: Sticks and stones may break my bones, but words will never hurt me!" She followed this lesson with a reminder.

"We will not tolerate fighting. God hates evil doers."

Naturally, fist fights were common among kids. The memorized litany did not always work. Bullies picked fights. Sometimes name calling was a process overlooked. Many fights were planned confrontations, ambushes. Anyone making a cutting, nasty assertion about another's mother or father worked to start fists flying. In this regard, my so-called "fight" occurred a few months after our family moved from Los Angeles city to the desert. Classmates I left behind referred to this move as going to the sticks. Justifications for making this huge relocation step was not to be made public. My parents said unbelievers would not understand. The reason they said was, "The Lord told us to move!" This was supposed to make a lot of sense, but it did not.

The fact that we were in a new area, a new home, and new school, I found myself in process of establishing a brave reputation. Showing coolness put me in an unfortunate situation. In a conversation with two new junior high school acquaintances an unexpected thing happened. We had started talking about speech habits and comparing walking styles. One boy made the typical childhood declarative challenge.

"You must think you are tough just because you come from L.A." For a moment I was taken aback. "What are you talking about?" I quizzed.

"Well for one thing you walk with that hitch in your stride. Cool guys walk like this, but guys who really think they be bad asses walk like this." He demonstrated the quick foot-dragging-hitch walking style and then contrasted the slower manner. We all laughed. I caught his drift and answered. "That isn't the way I walk and you know it. Jeez you're funny." Then the older boy cut the humorous moment short commenting on my manner of speech.

"Man you must be some kind'a Oreo or something. Listen to the way you talk. Trying to sound like white people. You say 'No it is not or isn't', instead of naw or ain't. You ain't white!"

This remark blindsided me. I had not seen this coming. I did not know that street language was a mark that distinguished those not in the mainstream. My school buddies in Los Angeles all talked the same way. I tried to justify why using plain correct English was not any act.

"Well, this is the way everyone in our family talks. We are not allowed to use sloppy English. You would understand if you spent just one minute in my house. Anyway, my parent say you can't get a good job if you talk like you live in the streets." The two boys stared at me for a moment in silence. Then the older one changed the topic to parental authority.

"So, your father is the boss in your house? I bet our father can beat up your father". This was traditional nonsense banter. Then conversation shifted to husbands hitting their wives.

The bone of contention soon became that my father, if he was a real man, had beaten my mother. In the parlance of the Black community, this is what men did. Naturally, I protested this conclusion. I was certain my father had never struck our mother. And judging from their loving relationship, her constant state being pregnant, I could not imagine violence between them.

This discussion took place on the basketball courts, of *Benjamin Franklin Junior* High School. I faced two well-dressed, caramel skinned brothers who from appearances were from "good" families. I protested vigorously.

"Real men do not strike their women. My father doesn't!" But both brothers disagreed.

"Oh yes they do! Man, your dad must be pussy-whipped!"
"That's not true!"

"Oh yeah? You calling me a liar? Then we're going to fight." Boom! A hard punch was delivered to my stomach, I went down. "Stay down! Stay down! "

Those were the next words I heard. This advice came from the younger brother. His older brother had struck me, and the argument ended with one punch. It took over a minute before I could even stand up straight. This fight was over, as was the arguing. From this I learned, sometimes it is best to strike first. Lost was the issue, whether my father ever hit my mother. I had lost a trivial verbal argument. It only took one quick sucker punch. I staggered half- kneeling, gasping for breath. I was thankful that no one else was there to witness my defeat. No one could side with me. And I dared not cry.

Our fight was short lived after the "bread-basket" stomach punch. This was new, as well as, a complete surprise. I was down on my knees in a flash, gasping for air almost five minutes. Not cool. I had unsuccessfully argued. From that moment on I knew that readiness for surprise attacks was a survival requirement. I must stay alert. I also learned that perhaps many, if not most, of my peers had seen their fathers strike their mothers. But my father had never raised his voice at mom. Dad was not a bully.

*****

While attending college I was having dreadful nightmares. At night in my dormitory bed, I sometimes would awaken crying and kicking the concrete wall. The target of my anger was my father. I struggled to undo his controlling grip. I had stopped shedding tears a long time ago. By this I mean, I had not cried since my childhood. As an adult, when news that each of my parents had passed away, I did not cry. By then I had no tears left, for loss, regret, or anger. I had even half-convinced myself that what my father said was true, real men did not cry. Dad said, Real men took it. Whatever happened, you had to cope. Crying was a wasted emotion. So, over the years I thought myself having a heart of stone. I became somewhat proud and fascinated with this self-ascribed moniker. I had faced great, heart rending disappointments and setbacks, but seldom ever brought to tears. This was true until three events in later years happened.

I saw my dad cry twice. The time when I was around twelve years old, he was having a nightmare. When much younger Dad had been my hero, a lifeline. My father told us how his father would swim out into the deep ocean for hours. His small head could be seen bobbing on the distant ocean horizon. Apparently, my dad had learned from his father the art of silence and avoidance. He told me on several occasions, there was a time to speak, and a time for silence. When grandpa died there was no fanfare at home. Barely a mention. However, when dad's mother passed away, dad's eyes seemed to be pools of tears that refused to spill out.

Another time for tears was an incident with the police. These were White men and it was clear they did not respect my father. At the age of eight or nine years old, I was holding my breath excited to be riding in the passenger seat. I felt proud because this was a late model car. My father and I were alone when suddenly strange lights flashed behind us. We stopped. Two white police officers emerged from their squad car, their hands resting on gun handles. The red and white lights continued flickering menacing warnings. The men approached our car which was a new *Kaiser, Henry J*, German made vehicle. One policeman demanded my father to show his drivers' license. His voice was stern and commanding.

"Just Keep one hand on the wheel!"

The other policeman stood on the side of our car where I sat, his .38 caliber revolver was out. I saw the gun muzzle point down toward the ground, and wicked gleaming bullet chamber. My father's voice was calm.

"Is there a problem officer?"

Dad politely inquired. but the response I heard was anything but polite.

"You be quiet. We will ask the questions!" was the response. One policeman began his inquisition.

"Where do you think you are going? Where did you get this car, did you steal it? Where do you work? How much do they pay you to work over there?"

This line of questioning was suddenly interrupted by the sounds of glass breaking behind me. The police officer on my side was now behind our car examining the accidental damage.

"Get out", commanded the policeman closest to dad, "take a look at this!"

My father slowly got out of the car and examined the broken taillight. One policeman explained.

"We're going to just issue you a warning ticket. You'd better get this fixed. The next time we stop you, there will be a fine to pay. You understand? And from now on, boy, you outta take a different route home."

Later, tears rolled down my father's face as he drove home brooding. I feared his irritation and tried to maintain the silence. Talking was risky. Finally, I marshalled courage to ask one question.

"Daddy, why did those men stop us?"

He was silent for a long while then softly replied:

"Those men need Jesus. Just pray for them." This was the stock answer to most queries.

I would pray alright. Maybe god would send lightning bolts from the skies. Or, maybe something would drop on their heads and make them become mere smudges. Revenge from god seemed like a good punishment. But there was no more mention of this incident. There need not be, because I remembered that my father punched my brother for questioning him too much. Merely looking at him with direct eye contact, sometimes triggered his volcanic eruption. Worse transpired if the question was uncomfortable or inconvenient. If dad said, "Don't you dare question me! What did you say?" I knew it was shut up time. My father was bigger than those two mean White cops who had been disrespectful. They had guns. Still it was obviously fool hardy for me to even remotely challenge his authority. His words were our law. In his eyes we would always be just naïve kids. Easily buffaloed. My older brother had the worse end of the bargain, perhaps somewhat due to my fierce loyalty to please our father. I was learning to become a chameleon of sorts. A young naive enabler.

CHAPTER 4

FAMILY BLOODLINES

[1952] **My parents preached against social welfare and handouts** yet they swallowed their pride, during holidays, when boxes of food from anonymous donors appeared on the front porch. Our family of seven was considered largest in the neighborhood. I was simply happy we had invisible heroes looking out for us. Angels lurked in the real world. When grand dad, my father's father and grandma, came from New York for a visit, I knew this must be true. During this brief intermission I received no whippings. Angels or magic were real. Grand dad would sit on the back porch, whittling on a small piece of wood with a small, worn pocketknife. I stayed some distance away because he was a stranger in our home and very soft spoken. One day I heard him softly singing.

"When the roll is called up yonder,

when the roll is called up yonder,

when the roll is called up yonder

I'll be there."

I was curious about what the song meant, so I crept a little closer to this strange man asked.

"Grandpa, what does role mean? Where is yonder?" His answer made a lot of sense to me at that time. "Son, the role is when God's voice calls you to heaven. You leave this world for more riches in paradise." My mouth must have hung open, because he gave me that stern look with his piercing gray eyes. It was the same regal stare I seen in old black and white photographs of him sitting wearing a black tailored suit and tall, black, stovepipe hat. Grandma, dark skinned, and attractive, stood close beside the chair exuding a mysterious air. Grandpa was the king.

They were followed by legendary tales of being punishers, skilled wielding a long bull whip, or cutting with the Cat-O-Nine Tails. After a long pause, he added. "Just be sure ta obey ya folk, an ya hear God's call. Otherwise, ya be forced ta meet de devil. On de earth ve call must vait for our ship ta come in. But ven ve die everybody git a ship o' treasures." Straining to capture meaning behind his island accent, I was a bit perplexed by his answer, but I knew something a pirates, ships, and treasures. In my mind I could see boxes of golden coins, sparkling necklaces, jewels, and large horns full of delicious food. I started to plague grandpa with more questions, but he simply leaned his head back, closed his steel colored eyes and dozed off. From his general stern demeanor and rigid jawline, I knew that he was too serious to indulge in more childish questions.

Grandpa was a tall, well-built, yellow skinned, clean shaven man from the Caribbean. Johannes Baltezar Vessup, Senior was a West Indian, born in 1893, on the island of St. Thomas. Although there was some discrepancy about the accuracy of this particular island being his actual birthplace. The Island of St. John's was marked by the well-known Vessup Plantation where a slave rebellion took place. However, grandpa worked the docks as a stevedore and was reputed to have spoken seven languages. On my first visit to St. Thomas and Haiti, the name Johannes Vessup, surprisingly, was well known by locals. I was more surprised when dad gave me new information in our rare quiet time chats. "You should easily be able to swim. When I was a child, your grandfather would take me to *Conney Island*, in New York. He swam for hours in the Atlantic Ocean. I could barely see his head far away. It was like a tiny dot on the horizon until it disappeared. He was very strong." This was dad's encouragement to me after he learned I had almost drowned in the high school gym swimming class. It had taken me that long to try to learn swimming. Living in the California desert there was no water nearby. Public swimming pools had limited days that allowed Blacks to enter. Waiting for one's ship to come in, was an expression my father often used when talking about future changes of fortune. We all had different meanings for this expression. I have no idea how or when my dad's parents came to America. However, this was where three of his five sisters were born.

The only other man-to-man boyhood chat I had with dad was when he would reminisce on his adventures in the U.S. Navy. Dad was comfortable with the ocean because he had been stationed on an Aircraft Carrier. He would talk about grown men crying and praying when mountainous waves tossed that ship like a rag doll. The military Aircraft Carrier was over three city blocks long, like a small village. His repeated stories touched on how men behaved after embarking on the beaches in the Philippine islands. Claiming the men acted like children, running toward the palm tree covered hills screaming and yelling, "We're gonna get some Japs! Whaaaaa-Hoooo!" He would say. "If there had been any enemy Japanese hiding, they would never have captured them, because the Navy guys were like sitting ducks." I enjoyed hearing those stories but was also scared by his description of Philippine women. He said, "Whenever we had Shore leave, men would pile into town to let off steam. Those women would grab and pull desperately at the men. A woman grabbed my arm telling me she would show me a good time. Her face looked like a death mask. Scared me. The fear of catching the Clap or Gonorrhea from her touch was real. I stopped going on shore leave after that. I stayed on board the ship and practiced playing my trumpet and the piano."

Dad also recalled how before being drafted into the armed services, he was often invited to play piano at an attractive Italian girl's home. He said, "We sat on the piano stool together as I played. Her strong garlic smells were over-powering, it was difficult for me to breathe.

Concentrating on the sheet music was almost impossible." Hearing those stories repeated, I deduced that Dad did not like foreign women. He said his ship came in, during the Fall of September 1945. This was when he met our mother-to-be in Los Angeles after being discharged. The Japanese had surrendered. My mother was half Black, half Cherokee Indian.

*****

My childhood hero was actor Sidney Portier. The adults around me looked up to him. Portier was from the Caribbean, like my father, and I often wondered why my father did not exhibit the kindness and patience conveyed by Portier. One thing they shared with their icon was personal dignity and a fierce since of pride. Both of my parents preached, "We work for what we get. A man is not a man if he cannot prove himself worthy of respect."

During this time, I was a child on tilt. Some said I had an evil streak. My life consisted of waiting each day for another invisible shoe to drop, physical punishment followed. According to my parents, Jesus was coming back, and the world would soon end. It was a whipping today, or the lake of fire tomorrow. The sundown was routinely followed by a whipping.

I decided that one way to win my parents' approval—or at least my mother's—was to eliminate the small, furry creatures she so hated: cats. I started by trapping the cats near the hot incinerator. The first time I got one, I grabbed its small, furry, frightened body by the scruff of its neck. It trembled as it hung from my hand, and its eyes revealed fear as it clawed at the air with stiff outstretched legs. In a way, I identified with its feeling of trapped helplessness. I, too, was helpless and clawing for relief and affection from my family. But there had been no relief, no affection—only doom.

I opened the metal oven door, felt the hot rush of hungry flames licking my face, and smiled. The cat in my hand would soon leave this sad, unfair world. I would be doing God's will. I felt no compassion.

Eventually, killing animals become easier for me. If such deeds are deemed necessary, then they should be done. Perhaps I did have a mean streak. I tortured insects and killed four- legged creatures with no emotion. For me, these were normal behaviors.

Genetics influenced both physical behaviors and mental traits, thae was certainly true in my family. We all bore physical traits that showed we were related: our head shape, the slant of our eyelids, our sensuous lips, an ambling walk, and a quirky boisterous laugh. The Vessups were all also musically inclined and loved to sing. Other shared family traits gave me more than a few reasons to be concerned about my mental health.

On my mother's side of our family was trouble. One small family secret involved Uncle Gene, a Craven, grandmother's first son of two boys. He was not a Vessup. Being a Craven, he had spent several years in Camarillo, the California state mental institution. Eventually, he was under the court-ordered supervision of our grandmother. Rumors held that Uncle Gene, the first son, had just acted crazy to avoid the military. Others claimed one of his fellow nightclub musician colleagues had been envious of his saxophone skills. This evil character had slipped some drugs into his drink one night, which nudged him over the edge. Either way, at some point, Uncle Eugene changed. I only had brief contact with him. When visiting Granny's, the adults took great pains to keep him away from us children. It was as if he had some contagious disease. Delilah Cravens, my mother's mother, was full blooded Cherokee Native American.

Her husband, an African Prince, had died committing suicide. This was the big family secret, as well as, dispute. There had been claims our mother's father had died an alcoholic.

In my youth, I wondered if one or both my parents had somehow become increasingly mentally unhinged. Whipping us and demanding that we thank them for so doing seemed insane. Their claims that this abuse was acts of love seemed even stranger. I wanted to get to the root of our family's strange dysfunctionality.

My father, Johannes, Jr., claimed he had visions and heard God's voice speak directly to him on many occasions. This may have been because he frequently fasted. Or, perhaps he was a tad schizophrenic. He prized order and discipline at home and in church above all else.

My father was a military veteran, a highly skilled tradesman and musician, and a socially likeable personality. He was also zealous about his religious faith. He was tall, muscular, dark, and handsome, and he seemed bent on proving to all the heights of his virility.

As his second son, I was dutiful, loyal, and committed to pleasing him. My mission was to make him proud of me. I feared him intensely. I watched him and listened to his every word. If I failed in this, I paid dearly.

One time, our family went to visit to dad's parents in New York for a weeklong national church convention. Mom and dad disappeared most of the time for long spiritual meetings; my two younger siblings at the time stayed with dad's sister, Aunt Christine; and my brother and I stayed with our grandparents. When my parents left for the day, my father said to me, "I want you two to get along. Listen to your older brother. Don't cause any trouble."

All went well the first two days, but I felt antsy and trapped in the small, stuffy apartment. The close smell of old age and hot moldy clothes choked me, and I longed to go outside in the fresh air. For the most part, my brother and I remained indoors reading or playing board games, but sometimes my quiet mysterious New York Grandmother sent me to the neighborhood store for treats like ice cream bars, or chips. Her directives were short and barely above a whisper. They never dispatched my older brother. He was content to stay inside with a book. Emboldened, one day after running errands, I made a request.

"Grandma, can I go play basketball downstairs with those kids?" I pointed out the window at the playground. She surprised me with her answer. "Sure. Just stay in my sight." With much gratitude I gushed a hurried thank you heading toward the door.

The voices of the elderly couple was audible. I could hear grandpa's broken English. "Vat ya' goin do lettin' de bye leave again? Dat be askin' for trouble ye know." And the New York Grandma's reply.

"No need to stayin' couped up inside." "What say?"

"He okay."

"Das dat."

I quickly closed the door and was gone. It felt good to be free even though I knew there were eyes watching me beyond that playground.

On a few other days, they allowed me to go to the playground downstairs to join basketball games. These adventures involved taking four flights of stairs down or riding in the smelly elevator. I had fun playing hoops and talking with kids my age.

After one particularly fun game, I returned to the stuffy apartment and conveyed my excitement to my brother. He was not interested in things outside and snapped, "Oh, shut up. That's nothing. You need to read a book."

"You shut up," I countered. "You can't tell me what to do."

"Well, I am. Read the Bible or something and be quiet."

"Make me. You're not my boss."

"I am the boss. Daddy told you to listen to me!"

"You're not!"

"Am too!"

Eventually, our bickering voices rose in volume. Our grandparents quieted us, and we gave each other the silent treatment for the rest of the day. However, the moment our dad returned, there was a huddle of adult voices conferring in the hallway. Then, dad appeared and boomed, "Aaron, is it true that you and your brother had an argument?"

"Yes, sir. He said he was my boss and—"

The next thing I knew, a horrible pain split my head, and I saw red, blue, and white stars.

My small body spun high in the air, and I felt weightless. After two complete revolutions, I landed on my knees. Everything was black for several seconds. In a daze, I heard my father's feet tread away and his voice quietly reminding me, "I told you to listen to your brother."

This seemed supremely unfair. I had more responsibility than he did and was often dispatched on errands. Yet I was deemed inferior due to birth order and age. After this episode, I resolved to never obey my brother in anything. I was furious with him.

At the same time, all I felt toward my father was fear and resentment. He was a master at using fear and punishment to get us children to obey him. Unfortunately, as time passed and I observed him more, this fear slowly changed to shame and disgust mixed with hate. I began to dream about killing him through a variety of methods: fire, kitchen knives, guns. I wished my father dead. It was becoming increasingly clear that if I did not leave home, I would not survive.

*****

My mother, Ellene Ernestine, was an attractive woman with smooth, caramel-colored skin, long black hair, and dark brown eyes. She was tall, and her shapely figure was a natural magnet for the male gaze. She was also under great strain. Her behavior seemed guarded and cautious. Her perfect teeth, only occasionally allowed gentle laughs to escape her full lips. She was proud but also a tad shy, except when singing before large audiences.

Her profession as a licensed beautician kept her in contact with the fashion-conscious, and her salon was a hub for other attractive women and wannabes. The hair salon was only one element of her popularity, as she was also sought after for her vocal skills. I frequently heard praises about her voice. Fellow mezzo soprano Marian Anderson was her opera-singer idol.

But by the time I was five years old, she was almost constantly pregnant. She sang less, and her dramatic mood swings made her unpleasant to be around.

Over time, my dad felt that his role as a provider was undermined by his wife working.

Her profession was suddenly a problem. Eventually, his demands that mom work at home prevailed. Many of her customers followed her, but dad could not stand the acrid odors of burning scalps and hair oil when he returned home at the end of the day. Soon, he forbid her from having customers in the house. Her life was reduced to resting in bed, practicing singing arias for weddings, reading *McCall* magazine, and dragging me along on shopping trips. When she had the energy, she bought the latest-fashion dress patterns and sewed. The resulting masterpieces vaulted her to center stage after church services every Sunday.

My parents took great pains to keep us away from the kids in our own quiet neighborhood. As a result, the majority of our playing occurred in the confines of the school playgrounds, where we could socialize freely during recess. But at home, interacting with those who didn't attend our church was frowned upon. Mom and dad routinely defended this decision, declaring, "Playing with unbelievers is letting the Devil use your mind. It won't hurt you to play inside your own yard. You can play at home!"

Kids on our block would knock on our door, asking, "Mrs. Ellene, can Johannes and Tony come out and play softball with us?"

Mom would answer, "Sorry, they have their own backyard. Why don't you play in yours?"

Others came by, asking, "Mrs. Ellene, can your boys join us in the roller derby skate group train?"

She'd respond, "Sorry, they're busy doing chores. Don't you have work to do at home?"

After a while, the neighborhood kids stopped knocking on our door. But they weren't dumb. Word got around.

"Your parents never let you come out to play with us."

"You must think you're better than we are. So holy. Too good for us, huh?"

Once in a blue moon, I was allowed to play 'Cops and Robbers' or 'Cowboys and Indians' with the boy next door. His name was Tony, and he was two years younger than me. His father, George, was a light-skinned police officer with short crinkly hair, and he often smoked a pipe while watching us play. His wife, Melrose, got along with our mother. She was also very light- skinned and pretty. She straightened her hair with a hot iron, just like my mother. Both George and Melrose "passed" for being white. A casual observer would need very sharp eyes to detect their racial origins.

Disgusted by this encapsulated lifestyle, my fear and sadness gradually grew into hatred, and I started to wonder about my own mental well-being. I felt ostracized and imprisoned and had to walk on eggshells within my own prison. My parents forced me to behave as if I didn't like people whom I liked. Earning parental approval came from mimicking ideas and attitudes they nurtured, whether I agreed with them or not. The fact that I now was dreaming about killing my father indicated to me that I was becoming unhinged. This notion was especially apparent when I commenced killing cats to win my mother's praise.

As our family grew, I noticed disturbing tendencies and behaviors in my siblings. Some seemed like they might be even more disturbed than I was. My sister Lollie had long conversations with imaginary friends well into her teens. She claimed I could not see her invisible friends because they did not like me.

In time, I decided to set a torch to our parents' bedroom— revenge for the countless whippings I had received. Unfortunately, my plan went awry when Lollie found the wooden matches in my secret toy stash and told our parents.

The heavy atmosphere of dead, gloom, and doom persisted in our home. My eventual departure from the family was eminent, and I developed a fierce desire to travel. I needed to claw my way out of this situation somehow. And I also knew I needed to worry about losing all my marbles in the process.

CHAPTER 5

Conditioning Nature

"Prepare for me! Prepare for me!"

My father's booming voice usually entered the house before he did. The king was inside the house. Next came the scent of work sweat. He worked in attics and crawled under buildings to install the rudiments required for modern technology. Sometimes he smelled like a peculiar mix of dirt, burnt hair, old lady's perfume, and rotting human flesh. Only after I caught his scent did my father's large frame loom through the kitchen door at the back of the house. At the sound of his truck engine arriving and shutting off, our vocal chorus had already sent a loud harmony singing "Da-a-a-d-e-e-y's Ho-o-m-m-e!" alerting all. But all was silent when the house door opened and closed. The giant was inside. We held our breaths. Then came these terrible words.

"Prepare for me!"

His heavy tread on the linoleum-covered floor indicated my father's whereabouts. Dad was a tall, intimidating man with thick oaken legs and granite-like fists. The abrasive cracked surfaces of his palms felt like sandpaper. He referred to his hands as 'God's hammers.' He used them to both beat me and to evoke beautiful melodies from the small cherrywood piano in the living room.

What would his mood be today? Playful or mean? It was hard to predict, but I could always tell from the tone of his booming voice and the tread of his first few steps inside the house.

"Prepare for me!"

This warning always sent shivers through my body, especially if my brother and I had argued again that day and interrupted Mom's afternoon sleep. Usually, my brother and I argued about trivial things, like what goes faster: a homemade skateboard or roller skates. But even silly arguments meant trouble.

My father's unpredictable entrance each day had me on pins and needles. Even if Johan and I hadn't argued, we'd still be required to play our piano lessons for an impromptu recital. For me, this meant I was still likely to receive a whipping. My performances were indisputable evidence that I had not practiced, which was an unforgivable offense in my father's eyes.

Practicing piano seemed like torture in and of itself, and I would much rather be whipped quickly rather than having to sit stiffly an hour suffering at the keyboard.

"Prepare for me!"

These words triggered fear. Certain smells could also induce fear.

There were also smells that reminded us of past happiness or foretold good things to come. Collard greens and chitlins (pig entrails), burnt buttered popcorn, shoeshine polish, barbershop leavings of curly black hair clippings, hot curling irons combined with burning hair grease, the braised skin of human scalps. There were the scents of new clothes for the first day of school, of Thanksgiving turkey dressing, cinnamon spice, and pumpkin pies. We were constantly reminded that food and shelter was proof of our parent's love for us.

I hated Friday nights because the weekend meant hours of kneeling on cold concrete floors. I became intimately familiar with floor smells from either praying at church, doing chores at home, or working with my father. There were the scents of carpet naps and fine, gritty dust on sharp metal venetian blinds. There were funeral flowers, wedding flowers, and the smells of death. There was the scent of cigarettes on threadbare carpets and moldy curtains.

There were human body smells: *Yodora* deodorant cream; *Murray's* hair pomade called axel grease by many, guaranteed to hold coarse, unruly hair in place; *AllSpice* aftershave lotion hurriedly splashed after sports competitions.

There were also the sickening smells of long car rides: burnt oil and fumes from vehicular exhaust. When the older kids were packed in the back of dad's pickup truck, we were pressed under the plywood roof like sardines. The choking smell of pressed composite wood made me nauseous, and I often vomited after the long ride to church in the countryside.

Dad had a ritual of anointing all church visitors' foreheads with olive oil that had been blessed. A few folks were afraid and showed their reluctance by frantically backing away, declaring, "He ain't gonna put that stuff on me! No way!"

Over time, dad's ritual transitioned into his comical habit of dabbing olive oil on automobile tires. He insisted God had told him to anoint the wheels of all cars that drove into the gravel church parking lot: "You may not believe this, but I have heard God's audible voice just as clear as you and I are talking now.

Many saints from other Pentecostal churches laughed at him, saying: "He's really taking his faith too far."

"Man, that brother is going off on the deep end."

"Yeah, he's out there alright. I ain't ever heard no voice from rocks or trees talking to me."

One day, the police showed up at our apartment. Two marked squad cars parked in front of our building, and armed uniformed men knocked on our door. "Your son is not under arrest or anything. We just need to ask him a few questions," they assured my mom.

Apparently, Johan had not been able to keep his eyes from invading some guy's privacy, and the guy retaliated by knocking my brother out cold.

Our parents did not want to press charges against the guy. In fact, they took the whole thing extremely calmly. They simply saw it as a sign to hasten our move to San Bernardino. We quickly moved away from Los Angeles.

My beginnings were humble and not in a hospital. I was born (an Aries) in a house on Vernon Avenue in Los Angeles, California in March 1947. Early on, it seemed something wasn't right with me. At first, my parents were worried about my "irregular" heartbeat. This concern continued for years, in spite of the fact that I physically outperformed peers. As I grew up, my drooping left eyelid caused self-consciousness about my appearance. Being called "Sleepy" or "Droopy-Eyed" by classmates were not compliments. I spent hours in front of mirrors trying to train my weaker eyelid to open wider. In my adolescent years, I suffered two life-threatening head injuries.

Though my beginnings were humble, they were not impoverished. We did not live in the "hood" or a slum area. I grew up in a new development of ranch houses located in south-central Los Angeles, on the fringes between Compton and Watts. There were no vagrants, gangs, or drug addicts hanging around. Homeowners embraced the middle-class values of dignity and orderliness. Homes were all well-kept, yards were carefully manicured, the streets were clean, and all cars were parked either in garages or on driveways. Trash was burnt in backyard incinerators, and small garbage cans were placed curbside only on designated days.

Our neighborhood was fairly a safe place. Occasionally, we heard stories of kids being kidnapped, so talking to strangers was frowned upon. One time, some kids stole a few of my dad's homing pigeons as a prank, but the birds returned. However, safety inside our home was another matter entirely.

I heard many stories of how my dad's parents were quick to use a bullwhip to punish him and his eight sisters. My grandfather often spoke of suicide squads in his childhood home in the Caribbean that fought against the Europeans. Now, in our household, just the thought of having been wronged brought havoc. The Devil bore the blame for any problems. However, researchers claim

Intellectual Disability (ID) affects three percent of the general American population. Signs of ID are limitations in adaptive skills, frequent mood swings, problems with basic communication, aggression, self-injury, and problems with self-direction. This disorder is genetic, so I had cause to worry. Most of my childhood I felt like I was walking on eggshells, juggling three shoes, waiting for one shoe to drop.

Physical thrashings were almost daily aspect of my life growing up. My parents often told me that I lacked self-control. Thinking that gaining my parents' approval would end these beatings was a misplaced assumption. Early on, I tried to run away both mentally, and physically. When things seemed particularly unfair, I would daydream about escaping and later took up running as a form of temporary escape to find mental clarity and balance. School was my only true haven, and my teachers were my angels.

For me, my life at home resembled the bigger picture of life in the wider world for black Americans at the time. In a culture that was filled with prayer, whipping seemed like a natural part of our religious routine. Both of my parents beat me while saying things like:

"You're special. We're doing this for your own good." "You'll thank us later. Don't let the Devil use you." "This hurts us more than it hurts you."

"Life was not meant to be fair. Suffering is something you need to be able to take."

I wasn't the only one in our family to be treated this way. My older brother, Johannes III, was tall, frail, wire-thin, and had the face of innocence itself. He earned top grades in school and was so well-behaved, other black guys called him names like "Momma's Boy," "Sissy," or "Pocahontas." Girls greeted him by yelling, "Hello, Proper!" He stood out at school by playing jump rope with the girls. His gait was not that of a gangster. He walked with a smooth glide, his back straight and head upright. He hated sports and continually worried about how to talk to the smart girls who liked him. This attraction was due to his ability to play advanced piano pieces. He should have been our parents' darling in every way, yet for some reason, my dad did not like my older brother. Perhaps it was due to Johan's softness, which is not exactly a quality expected of a black man's son. Whatever the cause, he seemed to irritate our dad by his mere existence. Tension constricted the atmosphere whenever they tried to discuss anything.

"But Daddy, sometimes people make mistakes. If these can be prevented through compromise, wouldn't that better?"

"Compromise? So now you're going to throw big words around? You think being in school makes you smart? Here, in my house, there is no compromise. What I'm telling you is in the Bible. You forget that I'm your father, and when I tell you to do something, you do it. Be obedient. If you honor me, you will obey, even if you think it's wrong. You're too young to see far ahead into the future. That's what parents are for. Disobedience is going against God's will, and you thinking and acting contrary to how I tell you is letting the Devil use your mind. There is no compromise!"

"Yes, Daddy. But my teachers say we should at least talk about our differences and—"

My father cut him off. "Don't you 'Yes, Daddy' me. You heard what I said! No 'But's. I don't care what your teacher says. You're either with me or against me. It sounds like you're trying to challenge me. You think you can challenge me?"

"No, Daddy. I'm just trying to say...*they say*, Planned Parenthood is—"

"Then shut your yap before I help you shut it. Humpf. You trying to school me? There is only one man here. Need I remind you again?" As he spoke, my father reached out from his position in the driver's seat to repeatedly slap my brother. Johan's body shook the frame of the 350 Ford pickup truck as he was thrown back against his seat and the door. When my father was satisfied that he had won the argument with his fists, he added, "Now I don't want to hear nothing about compromise. We are soldiers, and this is a spiritual war. There is no compromise with the Devil. Let this be a lesson you don't forget. You may think I'm wrong now, but you'll thank me later. You'll see."

With that, dad continued driving. He gripped the steering wheel, seething with anger.

He stared straight ahead as if in another place, completely forgetting where we were. Suddenly, he flashed an approving smile back at me. The look on his face told me that he had already forgotten what had just occurred. This smile reflected the same forgetful mix of moodiness and happiness I had witnessed on countless other occasions.

At home, he sometimes forgot that he intended to whip me after dinner. He would leave the dinner table and glance toward my bedroom down the hallway. I would still be there on my knees, my underwear off, my exposed buttocks still waiting for the whipping he had promised earlier in the evening when he had bellowed, "Prepare for me! It's punishment sho-o- w time! Fall in line and give up your behind!" I often had to wait in nervous agony for as much as forty minutes before he came to deliver on this promise.

Sometimes, seeing me naked, posed, and ready like that so long after he first gave his command made him smile or look confused. It even occasionally changed his mind on whipping. Most often, however, he would simply stride into the room and whip my naked body with enthusiastic relish as I held his thick ankles. His only explanation for this treatment was, "You've got this coming to you!"

Even his young daughters—my sisters—experienced the same maltreatment. My mother made him promise not touch the girls, but he often forgot this restriction. He'd had mental blackouts ever since his discharge from the Navy, and they were an unexpected plague in our family.

Our father, Johannes Baltezar Vessup, Jr., was a large, muscular man. He stood over six- foot-three and was 220+ pounds of solid rock. It was hard to believe he was called "String Bean" in his younger days. But I had seen an old photograph of him in full dress Navy blues. He had been a thin rail of a figure with a sheepish smile. His skin was a medium-dark chocolate brown, and his oval-shaped head was thinly covered by black hair slicked back with extra-heavy hair pomade. This hair style was called the Cab Calloway, and it was a fashionably old-school professional musician look. He had a prominent pointed nose, large calloused hands, a booming voice, and winning smile, which he readily flashed.

When he beat me, however, that smile was missing. Dad became the mad giant. His punishing weapon of choice initially was a wide, flat, leather tool-belt from the sagging pouch holding electrical tools. Later, He used a heavier automobile fan belt, which tore into my bare skin like searing fire. I could smell fear whenever he advanced on me carrying it. The scent would fill the room and mix with the scent of bath soap, Murray's hair pomade, and Vaseline hair tonic from my father's recent bath. "I'm gonna make you feel this," he promised, "and if you make a lot of noise, you're gonna get more. It's up to you. Take it like a man. You'll thank me later."

Fan belt lashes pounded and ripped my body for what seemed an eternity. Thick welts formed and blood flowed. By now, I had learned to grease my body before these whippings. I displaced my mind to ignore the physical pain. Locking my teeth into a tight clench, I focused on counting the blows. Sometimes I lost count and started simply listening to and analyzing the sounds the belt made against my skin. It was difficult not to yell and howl, but I did not want to give this giant monster that was my father the pleasure of making me cry. Sometimes, an involuntarily grunt escaped when the belt tip burned my scrotum. I could only hope he would soon tire from fatigue.

This was one of the many differences between my older brother and myself. Not only did Johan sing soprano, but when whipped he was a howler. He screamed non-stop during whippings, and the noise only further maddened the mad giant and fueled his energy. Often, the periods of torture he had to endure were further extended. In such instances, it usually took mom standing in the doorway and intervening to stop his beating. I hated the noise Johan made almost more than the pain of my own beatings.

Pain was something our father frequently talked about, accompanied by the reminder, "Real mean don't cry." He made it a point to often tell us about his military injury and long stay in a Naval hospital after being hit by a jeep. He gloated about conning nurses into believing he took their orders seriously. Fellow patients chaffing at female authority earned punishment that he avoided this way. His trip down memory lane inevitably ended with these words: "A real man takes what comes his way. He has a *can-do* attitude and copes. A man also takes what he wants. I am just doing my job and raising you right. I'm trying to make a man out of you. This is the Biblical way. You'll thank me later.

Our only respite from his beatings happened on the rare occasions when our mother intervened. Even though he never laid a hand on her, it seemed like she'd had enough. On such rare instances, she'd say, "Don't be so hard on him. He's just expressing his youthful energy. It's part of growing up."

"Well, I don't like that look on his face. I'm gonna teach him how I want him to grow up. There's only one man in this house!" my father would reply, but he's usually lay off after that.

However, on a few occasions, dad demanded that our mother join him whipping me in tandem. She was reluctant, as such physical abuse wasn't her way, but she also didn't want to be a disobedient wife. Afterwards, she would quietly apologize while rubbing ointment on my torn and bloodied body. She repeated over and over, "Honey, this hurts me more than it hurts you. Life is not supposed to be fair."

Our father taught us to believe that we were unique among other black Americans. Our roots were in the Caribbean islands of St. Thomas and St. Vincent. As West Indians, we would always be outsiders in the black community. It seemed like our family was an island of uncommon love. We were a strange family to our neighbors, a strange family in a strange church. I could only assume the kids on our block thought I was a strange, angry kid with a weird haircut.

I was always in a desperate search for ways to cope with the madness on my family. Writing poetry was secret, fun, and magical. My love of poetry started the day our father decided to enter a contest to win a car and started coming up with rhyming catchphrases. For weeks, my brother and I created jingles and rhymes, and these efforts won positive attention from dad when he came home from work. The goal of winning the contest ended when we discovered that the due date had already passed, but I didn't stop trying to find words that fit into rhyming verse.

I started writing rhyming verses in school, my one buffer from the terror at home. My early teachers offered a refuge through their warm, comforting, and caring communication styles. I focused on gaining their approval. I wrote a poem, "The Myna Bird," which earned adult attention and a California state award:

THE MYNA BIRD

There was a little Myna bird

So beautiful and black

Everything you'd say to him

He would repeat it back

If you'd chance to whistle

A lively tune to him

He'd wait for pretty girls to come

And whistle back at them.

This was in the early stages of having recognized being conditioned to behave in a particular manner. Humans were in a way like animals. Home was different climate than school. So, I always looked forward to going to school. It was heavenly escape. My third-grade teacher, Mrs. Peters, was especially magnetic. I often glanced at her while my classmates were engrossed in their assignments. She was both attractive and motherly, and I worked hard to win her attention and approval.

One day, when I completed my regular classwork early, she gave me a special project. I confided to her, "Mrs. Peters, I wish that you could be my mother."

She smiled warmly, but said, "That's not possible, because I already have a son your age."

After that, I ramped up my efforts to please her, hoping she would adopt me anyway. I wrote her short verses of poetry, but she simply accepted them with gracious smiles, saying, "Thank you. This is lovely." Still, I was happy that she so often rewarded my tendency to complete assignments early. She gave me a great many incentives to achieve, and the slightest frown or look of disapproval from her would break my heart.

On the other hand, older teachers Mr. Spite and Mrs. Birdell were quiet types who stuck to the standard regimen and repetition. They never raised their voices or became excited; calmness and balance were their standards. They had both taught my older brother and didn't seem to understand why I bristled angrily when they suggested I make him my role model.

My parents had also tried to compare us to motivate me, and I passionately hated the tactic. They peppered me with comments like, "Why can't you be like your brother?" "Your brother is a top student in every academic category," and "You should apply yourself more. Your brother is very smart, so you should be, too."

I didn't even attempt to hide how much these tactics angered me. I would scream back, "I am not my brother. I am not like my brother. Please stop assuming that I'm just like him," and become sullen in response. Eventually, those irritating methods stopped.

In addition to being sweet-tempered and academically successful, Johan was gullible and quick to please strangers, even the older Black guys who loitered at the edge of our neighborhood. I discovered this when passing a corner store one day. Some of these guys called out to me, "Hey you! Yeah, you! Come over here!" At first, I ignored these guys, but they were persistent. "Hey! I'm talking to you! I said come here!"

"No, you come here!" I countered, annoyed. I was a smart mouth, and though we had been taught to not talk to strangers, these guys were insistent. I couldn't resist talking back to them.

One of the bigger guys said, "Hey, ain't you Johan's little brother? Come 'ere! I got something for you!"

I realized I was out of my league and hurried my steps. "Don't make me come after you!" the older guy shouted.

"Well, if you do, I got something for you, too," I called over my shoulder and bent to pick up several rocks, arming myself.

Two of the guys crossed the street, coming toward me. I let loose one of the rocks in their direction, cocked my hand again for another onslaught, and continued to hurry away. They followed me for a few blocks, cursing, yelling, and hurling rocks and bottles of their own. I started to run, looking up and dodging their incoming missiles.

I told my mother about the incident. In response, she said, "At least you know how to take care of yourself. This is why I can't send your brother on errands. He takes too long coming home, gets distracted easily, and tells our family business to strangers. We don't want our business in the streets, you hear me? You should go to the other store, Vince's."

Vince's Liquor Store, in the opposite direction and lacking regular loiterers, was indeed safer—except for when mom sent me to buy sanitary napkins. This proved embarrassing because I didn't know that Kotex napkins are not for the dinner table or picnics. I scanned and searched store shelves forever, frustrated at my inability to find this item on my mother's note.

Finally, I reluctantly approached the cashier and showed him my mother's note with her preferred brand name and size.

"Hey, Ted," the cashier called out to his colleague with a laugh, "this kid is looking for sanitary napkins! Give him a hand. His mother's twat must be really huge!"

I never told her about being laughed at for buying sanitary napkins. Even after I knew what they were used for and where they were shelved in the store, I lived with this new wisdom in silence.

I loved sports in large part because I could impress my classmates with my athletic prowess. Any competition offered me a way to channel my anger. In both the classroom and on the athletic field, I felt free. I needed targets to direct my extra energy against. Even with sports as an outlet, I fought with my classmates a lot and was often sent to the principal's office for a paddling.

This tendency became particularly evident when I declared my love for the school's new teacher, Miss Gilliam. I wrote poetry about her dark springy curls and ringlets that bounced with each sumptuous stride. I wanted to kiss her caramel-colored face and light pink lips. Her smiles dazzled me, almost stopping my heart, and her mere presence set it racing. I was crazily in love, would happily confess this to anyone who asked, and was willing to fight for my love. I challenged and fought any male classmate who dared express romantic feelings for Miss Gilliam.

I wasn't alone in my adoration. Even the girls fawned over her. No one had any idea that among us boys, the competition for her unrequited love was fierce. The tug-of-war over the new teacher's affections continued an entire year. In class, we all strove to impress her with our intelligence, and outside class, we hoped she would wander close enough to us on the playground to see us playing hard. The poetry I wrote for her had not earned a public admission of affection, so I eventually devised a plan that I thought would be a fool-proof way to prove that Miss Gilliam belonged to me alone. I was compelled and blinded by an uncontrollable passion to impress her. Until, that is, reality struck.

By the time the ambulance arrived, the blood flow and the throbbing in my head had finally stopped. My head was cradled in Miss Gilliam's arms, and my face was close to her bosom. The delicate fragrance of her perfume tickled my nose, and I resisted the urge to sneeze. This was not a dream, but it felt like one.

I turned my eyes toward the emergency vehicle's long, low window. Two of my close friends were pressing their hands and faces against the glass between us, their expressions serious. I smiled and lifted two fingers in the "V" symbol for victory. I had won. Miss Gilliam had finally chosen me.

Suddenly, the ambulance driver addressed my teacher: "Ma'am, we're ready to go now.

The drive to the hospital will take only about six or seven minutes. Do you want us to turn on the siren?"

There was a moment of silence, then Miss Gilliam looked down at me with a gentle smile. "Oh, I don't know. I think we should ask him. Aaron, do you want to hear the siren as we drive to the hospital?"

"No, I'm okay. You can keep it off. I like it this way."

Miss Gilliam was so pretty at a distance. But now, up close, I could see that her skin was deeply pockmarked with small craters. Also, a line of hair above her top lip revealed a shadowy mustache in need of attention. The dark smeary mascara and runny black eyeliner around her eyes were like a deformed circus mask. Her breath smelled like rotten garbage, and the scent clashed with the perfumed delights on and beneath her blouse. I had never noticed these imperfections before, and my heart began to sink. I had never been this close to my crush before, and now that I was my disappointment was strong enough to block out the pain in my head.

Fourteen stitches and two months later, my father stormed into the kitchen one day waving a letter. "I just got a bill from the hospital. What's this about a seventy-five-dollar ambulance ride? Do you remember if they turned on the siren?"

"Yes sir, I remember. They didn't turn it on. I asked them not to. My head was really aching."

"Your head was aching? Well, mister man, your backside's gonna be aching soon. You had no business trying some silly trick on that gym set. Are you sure they didn't turn the siren on?"

"Yes sir."

"Well, you owe me. You're going to pay for this. When you get your first job, you're going to pay me back. I'm putting this is on the debt list. Bank on it!"

And that was that. I never saw Miss Gilliam again after the picnic for graduating sixth graders, but years later, after I received my first paycheck, my father claimed this and other debts I had accumulated over the years. I hated the reminder of my crazy youthful attempt to attract female attention. It should have served as my important life lesson, but over-checking myself is a twisted skill I had learned at home. I was locked-steeped in a household dominated by extreme emotions and crazy behavior. If anything, that failed first attraction, may have partially explained the events surrounding my first marriage years later.

CHAPTER 6

Gangs and Bullies

Years before my religious conversion, I felt tinges of jealousy whenever new classmates arrived. Mark Twain Elementary School seemed to be a magnet for immigrants and military brats. Exposed to more than the ten-mile radius of southside Los Angeles, these new students seemed worldly, and based on their fresh appearances, I could tell that their parents were financially well-off. In this environment, girls fawned over the new boys who arrived. I will confess to clenching my teeth from jealousy until my jaws were sore. I was not alone in shooting glares at the new boys. For our part, we boys feigned loyalty to our own girls, pretending that the cute new girls were no match for our veteran heart-throbs.

However, the day Mimi Hamilton arrived, this charade changed. The scales of social acceptability and cuteness went suddenly askew. Not only was Mimi smart like the rest of us in our special accelerated learning class, she was smarter. She dressed in impeccable fashions every day. Her long, tight braids were longer than the other girls'. Her skin was a light almond- cinnamon color that glowed like gold. Her perfect teeth flashed with proud confidence each time she answered our teacher's questions. None of us dared to admit we liked her, but there was trouble looming ahead.

Maybe it was because she was too perfect, too smart. It was clear the other girls in class would never warm up to her. We all thought she talked too much and was too quick to answer our teacher's questions. Perhaps she was an adult disguised as a child. The girls strove to keep her out of their closed social circle at recess, but Mimi outsmarted them and formed a clique of her own with other girls on the playground.

Mimi's coming taught me that being "new" came with challenges, as well as benefits.

Until then, I had naively craved the usual welcoming receptivity and curiosity shown to newcomers.

When Pedro Blanco joined our mechanical drawing at Enterprise Junior High, I learned that newcomers could face even worse treatment than being shunned like Mimi. Pedro was from Mexico and could not speak English, so he just smiled a lot. Our class was full of restless, naughty boys who came from several different area elementary schools, and it was clear that many of these kids had no interest in learning.

The quiet, bald, white teacher, Mr. Blandon, seemed unable to demand or even maintain order. He routinely turned his back and shiny bald dome on the class to write instructions on the chalkboard or fasten his eyes on a book on his desk. He rarely looked up even when spit balls plunked on the wall behind him. He was absent with his presence. The bad eggs in the class, led by J.P., a perennially well-dressed black youngster, knew just how far to take their misbehavior.

The morning Pedro Blanco joined our class, J.P.'s crew acted differently. There were no spit balls or rowdy conversation. Apparently, the bullies had a new plan in mind.

I had volunteered to help Pedro in Mechanical Drawing class, so he sat next to me. I gave him cues about how to use a protractor for certain assignments and when to use which type of pencil. Pedro was a fast learner, and the class period passed quietly. By the end, he seemed more at ease.

As our class of rowdy boys noisily waited for the dismissal bell, J.P. inched closer to the new kid from Mexico. Apparently, his silent sizing-up of our class newcomer was complete.

Before I knew what was happening, J.P. was standing directly behind the foreign outsider's stool, waiting. Mr. Blandon's head was bent reading, as usual. The sound of scraping stools, conversations, and muted giggles heightened. Suddenly, there was a pregnant pause, like the silence before a storm. Then it happened.

The moment Pedro stood to straighten something on his sloping desk, the impish J.P. made his move toward Pedro's stool. He was like a stealthy brown cat. A micro-second later, Pedro sat down on his stool again—and on the long thumb tack J.P. had placed there. Shock immediately registered on Pedro's face, and he sprang up from his seat, clutching his butt. Pain and surprise flashed across his reddened face. He howled loudly, but the sound of his anguish was drowned out by the clanging dismissal bell. The class erupted in gleeful laughter, and a flood of cheering boys rushed from the classroom. Pedro looked at me with tears in his eyes. He was no longer smiling. I felt bad for him and guilt because I had not realized this mischief was going to happen.

But the matter was far from over. A short time later, during the lunch period, I was summoned to the school counselor's office. Three other people are there: the counselor, an interpreter, and Pedro. All stared at me expectantly, urging me to confirm the identity of the culprit. After relating what I had observed, I returned to the lunch area outside the cafeteria. I sat alone on a low brick wall that separated the picnic tables from a grassy field where small groups of students threw Frisbees to each other, played catch, or engaged in flag-football games. I noticed a group of boys gathered at the far end of the picnic tables, all of whom were staring at me. One by one, these boys got up and trotted toward me in a single file line. The sight was curious, but I thought nothing of it.

Like antelopes, each boy hurdled over the low brick wall where I sat. They cleared the wall one-by-one. The last three runners passed much closer to me than the others had, and I recognized the last two: J.P. and his friend Monkey-Face Emmitt. When J.P. jumped, the breeze trailing behind him ruffled my shirt. Seconds later, Monkey-Face approached with an evil grin, and he grabbed my shoulder as he leapt over the wall. I tumbled backwards, falling onto the patch of grass and dirt below. My white shirt was now covered with dark dirt and grass stains.

Surprised, I jumped up quickly and started running after Monkey-Face as he sprinted away with his group. I stopped short when the entire group turned toward me, now banded together. They were waiting.

"Come on, punk," Monkey-Face Emmitt shouted. "You wanna fight us? Come on!"

I slowly walked toward the group. I knew this would not be a fair fight. I had to diffuse it now. I glared at the gang and pointed at Monkey-Face. "Coward," I shouted back. "I'll get you! I'm not gonna forget this!"

"Yeah, that's right! Don't forget this! We'll fuck you up just like we did your brother!

Come on! Come on," he called back.

I didn't take the bait and stood my ground. The gang laughed and walked away, moving further onto the recreation field. I was still in shock and had no idea what they meant by their reference to my brother, but it was clear that this had been retaliation for me backing up Pedro Blanco's story.

That evening, I told my brother what had happened. "What did Monkey-Face mean about 'fucking you up'?" I asked. "Did they do something to you? What did they do? Did you tell mommy and daddy?"

"Yeah, I told them, but I can't talk about it," Johan said. "Besides, whenever I tell mommy about how they pick on me, she says to just pray about it."

"Come on, man! Tell me something!"

"I can't, so forget about it. Just stay away from them. That's all I can say."

My brother had always been passive, but I was not one to let the matter rest. I had been dragged into the dirt and publicly embarrassed for sticking up for the foreign newcomer, and I would have my revenge. I resolved to keep an eye on J.P.'s gang and catch Monkey-Face Emmitt alone after school one day. For days, I carried two large rocks in my pockets and brought my handmade zip gun to school. It was small and easy to conceal. That gang would have a big surprise if they came near me again. Fortunately for all of us, J.P. had been expelled, and his gang more or less disbanded. I didn't see them gathered at lunchtime again.

Shortly after that, our family suddenly moved before the school term ended. There was no forewarning, and I didn't even get a chance to say goodbye to my friends. I had no idea that I would see Monkey-Face Emmitt again many years later when we were much older adults.

*****

Shortly before we moved away from Los Angeles, I awakened one night to the sounds of yelling, screaming, and loud bangs and crashes coming from the living room. The screams and pleas were from my mother, while my father's voice sounded like a woeful dying foghorn blaring between crashing waves and howling tears. My brother and younger sister were apparently still asleep and dead to the world.

Opening my bedroom door, I crept down the hallway and slowly peeked into the living room. The usual comforting smells of biscuits and pound cake were gone, and instead, the air was filled with dread, chill, and my parents' voices. Dad was in anguish. Mom was a scared, tearful cheerleader, calling out:

"Help him, Lord! Please, Jesus!"

"I am your faithful servant! I believe! I believe! I believe!" "Lord Jesus! Rebuke the demon. Help Lord!"

"The Devil is a liar! *Shamanan non shama*! Hallelujah *bestula pisto*!" "Praise god! Hallelujah! Victory is in your blood! Jesus! Jesus!"

"I rebuke the devil. I believe in the power of your blood! Shamana quatro! Shamana aloha!"

I had never heard my mother speak like this before. My parents were usually highly articulate people and did not allow sloppy English or slang words in our home, yet this sounded like a drunken auctioneer on speed pills. Later, I learned that this was called "speaking in tongues."

Widening the door crack, I could see my father, his mouth lathered and foaming. He tossed a table lamp to the opposite corner of the room, charged the large picture window, grabbed the heavy draperies, and yanked hard. He ripped down the curtains and sent the venetian blinds behind them crashing to the floor. He kicked the piano bench, and it flipped in the air like a feathery splinter of wood. Sheet music went flying as the seat opened like jaws spitting out paper. My mother sat on the edge of the long red sofa, both hands at her throat as she watched and wildly prayed. My father's eyes were closed, yet tears rushed down his cheeks as he vaulted around the large living room, bouncing from walls to windows. His arms swept the air as if trying to clutch something invisible. It seemed like my dad had gone crazy. I was terrified.

I wanted to say something. The word "stop" came to my brain, but no sound came out of my mouth. My throat was constricted with fear, and only a small gasp of air escaped. My mother must have heard me though, because her head turned toward me quickly. "Go back to your room," she ordered. "Don't you come in here! The Lord is dealing with your father. Go!" Then mother locked her eyes on my father again, and I became invisible. I knew it was best to make myself scarce. I didn't want my father to come to and see me there, watching him in his moment of darkness. This was adult stuff, and I had no business knowing about such things.

The next morning, we children sat in the warm kitchen and stared gloomily into our cereal bowls. I asked my siblings if they had heard anything during the night. No one had, so I decided to keep quiet about what I had seen.

Eventually, we learned that dad had earned the highest score on the state board examination, but his expected promotion was denied. His supervisor had simply told him, "It's nothing personal. Better luck next time!" This was the second time a promotion had gone to a less-qualified white person in his fourteen years with the county. This severe disappointment had occurred during a month of ritual fasting.

Dad never used words like "gay," "fairy," or "homosexual." Instead, he merely pointed out perceived faults, saying things like, "He's not a real man. His wrists are too limp to pull thick number-ten or number-eight electric wires. His walk is a bit feminine."

It was during this same period that the police stopped our dad while driving our new family car and purposefully broke a rear tail light. I knew dad was angry and watched his jaw clench as he stared ahead at the road with a stern expression. Those white policemen were like bullies on the playground. They were like kids wanting to have fun at someone else's expense. But I was a kid, and they and my dad were men, and even I could see how wrong this all was.

Dad became grimmer and meaner after this. There was no more smiling or whistling. He was never the same again. He started dabbing my head with olive oil before whipping me.

*****

The very idea of being forced to play baseball irritated my brother Johan to the point of dizziness. He actually even fainted one time when we were at Exposition Park near the Coliseum. Dad had brought along a heavy thirty-eight-ounce autographed Duke Snyder baseball bat and large twelve-inch softball. He wanted us to hit the ball as high in the air as possible. Dad said this would improve our coordination skills. I was overjoyed at the exercise. Johan fainted soon after we started.

My father later assigned the derisive label "he-she" to my brother, in part because he sang soprano in the school choir. Despite dad's dislike for his eldest son's mannerisms and interests, mom was protective of him and favored him in a great many things. Perhaps it was because he learned how to braid our sisters' hair and cut out dress patterns for her.

The deep freezer in the garage was large enough to store a human body. For years, it was almost always full of assorted steaks. Beside it were a Westinghouse washer and dryer. When either of these machines broke down, our dad had a fresh fan belt to use on me as a whip. None of these modern appliances accompanied us when we moved to our next house. Of course, dad's whips *did* make the trip.

One Christmas, a mysterious donor gave our family an electric bread maker. Sometimes this small machine would blow a fuse in our house or trip a circuit breaker, and we would have to reset the main electrical box or buy fresh fuses. We overlooked this inconvenience because we relished the scent of fresh bread that helped damper other unpleasant lingering odors.

I soon learned that it didn't matter where we lived or what we lived in. The world inside our walls was still a punishing, imprisoning jungle. Our parents seemed bent on teaching us to live a certain way. Desperate to escape, I yearned to learn more about the outside world. Our family slowly circled down the social drain. We fell from lower-middle-class suburban comfort to life in a cramped brown shack in the desert.

I watched the spiritual figures in our life with increasing suspicion and apprehension. Most of the adults in our cult seemed to be disfigured or physically challenged in some way, yet they fervently claimed that they were the only true children of God. I didn't want to look or act like them. I didn't want to own a house filled with hungry mouths to feed. I didn't want to sport a huge belly like my father. I saw no point in belonging to a group, to then be ostracized by that same group. As our small world became increasingly electrified with rules and prohibitions, all I could do was hope someone in our family did not blow a mental fuse. Even I was coming close to snapping.

CHAPTER 7

Trade Marked

I could barely breathe. Each inhalation could be my last. Helping dad with this electrical job found me in this situation. We were installing ceiling lights in a hot, airless attic. I was alone above the room and dad was below. Spatial clearance was limited to eighteen inches. My knees and elbows had long-since gone numb supporting my weight lying prone in this steamy, suffocating space. If this situation had been underneath a building floor, my face was usually inches from cool dry dirt. Attics were a different ballgame. Height meant hotter, especially in summer. Cottony materials called "spun glass" used for insulation was deadly. This material was useful keeping heat or cold inside living quarters. Installed in padded strips was seen in new constructions. Blown in like loose snow, by mechanical pumps was the old fashion process. Either way, just a few minutes of close contact breathing these materials was harmful to the lungs. I did not have a face mask. And prolonged contact made my skin itch. It was hard to not scratch. Often, I felt like I would suffocate.

"Hey! Don't go to sleep! I'll be handing the material in a few minutes!" That was my dad's way of checking on me. He did not I was okay.

"Yes, sir. I'm here." I knew better than to say I was tired or could barely breathe. Saving my breath, sneezing occasionally, and shallow breathing was all I could do to survive.

Working as my dad's "helper" was a clear call for loyalty, and I couldn't help but feel like a living sacrifice. If I were to die stuck in the cramped confines of this hot attic, no one would know except my father below. Furthermore, the silence from his long absence suggested a horrifying thought: he didn't even really care. Still, sons must obey their fathers at all costs. There was no getting around this reality, so I remained at this station. My ears were trained for the sound of my father's voice. I hoped he would return soon.

I already I felt as if I were dead and buried. Cobwebs and dead, dried-out spiders with stiff, spindly legs hung close to my head. The scents of dead wood and mold assaulted my senses. The small, distant porthole of a window at the end of the space let in a faint hazy light. Thick insulation pads called 'spun-glass' kept the heat in and the cold out and made the attic an oven-like prison. Powdery dust that had lain undisturbed for years covered everything.

I was growing increasingly worried. Had my father forgotten me? Had he become engaged in another of his Bible-thumping rants with the homeowner? If nothing else, it was clear that this electrical project was on-hold for the moment. God's work was always top priority.

I closed my eyes momentarily and tried to forget about the heat and my itchy skin. My dark-brown forearms were covered in a white sheen of salt from my sweat and the powder that was everywhere. I was tired and wanted to take a brief nap, but didn't dare for fear of accidentally punching a foot or knee through the ceiling and creating a huge hole. Dad would have had my hide for that, since it would mean that *he'd* have to pay to fix it. To my thinking, it was better to die in this suffocating attic than to live after a careless mistake.

I kept my breathing slow and imperceptible, as though I were playing dead. I dared not move and stir up more ancient dust. I wanted to inhale as little of it as possible. The urge to sneeze crept up my throat and tickled my nostrils. Sneezing would stir up even more dust, so I compressed my breathing, trying to resist the urge.

I slowly inched backward toward the open ceiling crawl-space cover. I could feel the fresh air rising in a wave from the room below. This was better than trying to reach the ventilation grid below the hazy glass window on the distant wall, and the risk of going through the ceiling was lower. My arm muscles ached and itched. My legs had lost their feeling. I tried to think about songs or about people at school.

My friends didn't know what I did on weekends. I rarely had the luxury of studying and doing homework on my days off, the way they did. Our family had to eat. Dad had to bring home the bacon, and he needed help to do that.

My older brother didn't work with our father. He simply didn't have what it took. The one time he came with us, he questioned dad about something vague while we were still in the truck. That was a big mistake on his part.

"Don't you question me! Just do as you're told," dad had snapped. Johan started to protest, and dad's fist shot out and connected with his firstborn son's cheek. My brother cried silent tears. The look of helplessness in his eyes hid his stubborn defiance. There was a moment of empty silence.

Suddenly, I had an idea. I opened the glove compartment on the dashboard. Inside was a small bottle of olive oil. I pulled it out and handed the sacred oil to my dad, respectfully saying, "Daddy, aren't you supposed to use this first... dab it on his head, I mean?"

He stared at me silently for several seconds, and a strange shadow crossed he face. "Put that back!" he said.

Johan never went to work with our father again. Perhaps he has his own strategy for survival in our house. He preferred to stay home with mom and help her iron the girls' dresses and braid their hair, rather than endure our father's punishment. In a way, he was free.

But I knew the right tools to bring when dad demanded them. I quickly returned from errands. Dad knew he could count on me for swiftness and accuracy. I did my best to prove my loyalty and obedience. This was the only way I knew how to show him that I believed in God. It was my only means of self-preservation.

But for the moment, I had to focus on breathing slowly and not becoming lightheaded. I didn't want to risk blacking out and waking up face-down on the soft, spongy insulation pads.

I just had to breathe. Whether, swimming, walking, playing, or even sleeping, unimpeded airflow kept me going. This was no different. Just breathe. Slowly. Breathe. Slowly, the wave of near-suffocating panic passed. I could hear my blood racing through my head. My eardrums pounded a steady tempo, and I heard a high-pitched ringing sound.

If Jesus returned to Earth today, I knew I would be saved, because I had remained close to dad, always listening and always obedient. At least, this was what I was told every time we went to church. I listened to sermon after sermon between the loud emotional praying, weeping, dancing, and shouting, "God was love!" I believed that everything that happened inside the walls of our church was sacred. My attendance grew to became nightly rather than once or twice a week. Even so, I felt like a mechanical robot programmed into a routine that I now detested.

In our church, I witnessed the process of mentally breaking people down over days, weeks, months, or even years. I learned the power of sleep and food deprivation. Regular fasts were rewarded afterward with good food and music. Food had never tasted better than it did after these long fasts. These acts of intense self-discipline were signs that we were God's people and that we knew His truth. We were the chosen few who knew the only way to Heaven. We committed ourselves to suffering while proclaiming for all to hear: "God is good!"

By the time I was nineteen, my parents' voices were constant and unrelenting in their warnings about my future:

"Jesus is coming. Are you ready? We love you and care for your soul. We agonize at the mere thought of you being lost."

"Do you really think you can stand a moment in the Lake of Fire that God has prepared for the unbelievers? Don't you want to be saved?"

"If you're gonna live in my house, you will serve the Lord."

"I ain't gonna have no Devil eating my bread and sleeping under my roof. If you think this, you'd better think again! You'll have to get with the program or leave!"

"You know we love you so much. Your father and I have a responsibility to save your lives and your souls. When we beat you, it hurts us, but we must follow the Scripture."

"Yep! 'Spare the rod, spoil the child!'"

"The Good Lord admonishes us to 'Present our bodies as living sacrifices,' so we're gonna do whatever it takes to make it in to Heaven. Whatever it takes. Even if we have to sacrifice one of our own because they let the Devil use their mind. I rebuke that Devil in the name of Jesus! Cast that demon out of him!"

But, again, preset moment, I just needed to breathe. My head felt thick and my mind, groggy. The shallow intake of air from my slow, slight gasps made my heart race. In my mind's eye, I had just run up a steep hill. My chest felt heavy. It was hard to get enough air. I ran toward what looked like a wooden cross. Was Jesus hanging there? The wind whipped around me, sounding like an eerie howl. The scent of mold blended with that of cooked onions and greasy fried meat. Suddenly, I heard a familiar voice from somewhere beneath me: "Lover! Oh lover, are you still with us? I brought you a hamburger. You can come down now. Let's go home."

I hated it when my dad called me "Lover." It always inspired strange questioning expressions on the faces of onlookers. Still, I joyfully descended from the cramped attic very slowly. It was difficult to keep my balance after so long in that stifling oven, balancing on cutting beams with sore knees. I did my best to hide this fact from my father so he wouldn't think I was weak. I silently prayed, *Please God, don't let me start sneezing. At least not where Dad can see me!*

CHAPTER 8

New Transition

O ne day, Miss Vi's apartment caught on fire, and people in the neighborhood speculated that she had tried to burn the entire apartment building down just to spite my father. He demanded rent paid on time, but she frequently had been late. Our parents owned a four-unit apartment complex. We were landlords. This was a spiteful label to those who barely scraped by at or below minimum subsistence. For weeks after the fire, a burning smell permeated our clothes. The fire inspectors eventually determined that Miss Vi had left the kitchen gas on while baking something, and there had been an explosion in her oven. She had been extremely lucky that the firefighters had arrived in time. I was jealous of the firefighter who had the envious task of carrying Miss Vi down the steep ladder. In his arms was his prize: our panty-less neighbor, clutching his neck and half-heartedly closing the front of her scanty negligee. I continued to nurse fantasies about her, even as I stood outside my burning home in the cold among curious onlookers.

Miss Vi wasn't the only woman I was enamored with. Two girls in my English class, Aletha and Mary, at Thomas Edison Junior High also held my attention. They were both pretty and smart. Aletha was an outspoken brown-haired black girl, and Mary was a quiet blonde white girl. Somehow, my classmates got wind of my attraction to both girls. Aletha's clique didn't like that I was even paying attention to Mary. To them, I had no business liking two girls, let alone one of them a white girl. They kept pushing me to make a choice.

Then, one of my male buddies presented me with a new diversion: Paulette. Paulette was dark, chubby, not that bright, and available to whomever, to do whatever. During school recess, my buddies and I would take turns hiding with chubby Paulette, between vacant bungalows fondling her large breasts. Those mounds stubbornly pulled at her blouse, where just two buttons kept joyful mounds of flesh in prison. That rack did not belong on an eighth- grader.

The mere thought of seeing those full, adult-sized, voluptuous tits with dark nipples excited me, and Paulette seemed happy receiving our sexual explorative attentions. Fondling her exposed breasts represented the height of sexual excitement for me at the time. I quickly forgot about Aletha and Mary. Two years later, this experience would come back to haunt me. By this point, we had moved out to "the sticks" of San Bernardino. My father had been elevated to pastor and leader of the Bethel Apostolic Faith Church, a Pentecostal congregation. I had become a "saint" and official church member. This conversion move meant that I no longer would be whipped. I was officially a child of God. There was no more devil inside me, as long as I followed orders. I functioned machine-like at home and church.

In his role as pastor, dad would hear "confessions" from church members twice a year. The problem with these confessions was that our mother also would sit alongside him. Should listen as people revealed their secret embarrassments, inner conflicts or transgressions. The logic behind this was that many of the single young ladies might have intimate things to say and might not feel comfortable discussing them with a man, though I sometimes wondered if mom was suspicious of their motives toward her husband. Either way, our mother sitting in on confessions was a problem for some, so much so that more than a few members stopped attending our church.

As for me, by becoming an official church member, I could now 'speak in tongues.' I now belonged to the Lord and was "SAVED." But this meant that my days of fighting were done and that my past life must become an open book. Confessions were now mandatory. And so, my parents eventually heard about my youthful escapades on the schoolyard with Pauline.

I don't think my father was shocked. His facial expression reflected a matter-of-fact "boys will be boys" attitude. My mother, on the other hand, almost fell out of her chair. "You did *what*?!" She leaned forward with a horrified look, her forehead creasing like a worn road map. "Repeat what you just said!"

"I said, we took the girl behind the vacant classroom building and tried to feel her up—"

"*What*?! You tried to 'fill-her-up'? And how did you two manage to do that?" Mom's question was so loud and frantic, I was certain other church members waiting in line several feet away could hear.

Confession was one of the worst things about membership in our church.

*****

Shortly after Miss Vi's apartment caught on fire, our family moved to a four-bedroom ranch-style house on a *Cul de sac*. This move was several steps up the social ladder and felt like heaven. The neighborhood was fairly new, with similar homes to ours. We still didn't have much privacy, though, since our neighbor's house was almost an arm's length away. I could look out my bedroom window and see into one of their bedrooms. When darkness fell and we had to turn the lamps on, there was little privacy. Indoor conversations could be distinctly heard from the street. In our case, loud praying and wailing from embarrassing whippings made its way out beyond our walls. I hated the fact that our lives were still under scrutiny.

In our first home on Crocker street, there was more space between the simple three- bedroom ranch-style homes. It was usually quiet, and the loudest noises heard outside our house were caused by a gang of six or seven kids on steel-wheeled roller skates roaring down the sidewalk. Occasionally, the sounds of happily cheering voices from street football or baseball games interrupted the quiet. For the most part, we were confident that the loud, fervent praying our father led us in and the cries of pain from his frequent tortuous whippings did not escape beyond our walls.

Still, the inevitable finally happened one night not long before our first move. Just after a whipping session, there was a knock on the door, followed by continuous doorbell ringing when no one answered. Eventually, my father went to the door, where Miss Irene, our next- door neighbor, was waiting with an attitude of fury. She had heard our cries of pain and was threatening to call the authorities if the noise did not cease.

Afterwards, my father paced the living room in a rage. "Who does she think she is? She's not qualified to judge what I can and cannot do in my own home. What does that woman know about family discipline, anyway? Nothing! She's not even married. She doesn't have a family. A man's home is his castle! She'd know that if she had a man."

"Yes, dear," my mother said, trying to placate him. "We never complain about her party noises." Miss Irene held parties in her home once a month. I was always intrigued by the wonderful smells of barbeque ribs or chicken grilling in her backyard. We never grilled or barbequed anything.

"She's probably just jealous of your singing," dad said. "She's the real problem here, what with all that ungodly drinking, smoking, and loud Devil music!"

"Oh honey, she doesn't mean any harm. People are just nosey, is all. It's their nature.

We should pray for her tonight. Maybe—"

"There's no 'maybe" about it," dad cut in. "I know the Bible tells me to 'train up a child' and use the 'rod of correction.' I'm just gonna follow the Bible, and I don't care what busybodies think. Even if we have to sacrifice one of our own, like they did in the Bible, I'm not gonna let nothing or nobody shake my faith. Our other neighbor is an officer of the law, and he's never tried to interfere when we discipline our children. He knows the law, too, but he's Christian. That's the difference. He's a man that understands."

"Dear, maybe we should think about moving," mom said. "Maybe this is what the Lord is trying to tell us to do."

Mom continued speaking softly and soothingly, and dad's anger slowly cooled, but I felt a chill run through my body. Was I hearing right? Did my father really mean what he said about *sacrificing* one—or more—of us? Was this their purpose in having a large family? After all, both of my parents often said, "I brought you into this world, and I can take you out! We have god's love for you!" This was a frequent litany as I was being whipped. I viewed myself as fodder, their sacrifice to God.

After this, I started having nightmares about our parents selecting one of us kids to sacrifice during the night. After all, I had heard stories at school about children going missing and being kidnapped. Perhaps kidnapping was just a cover story to explain the absence of kids who had been sacrificed to God by their parents. What I needed was more time away from home. Getting a job could make less church attendance justifiable.

CHAPTER 9

Tough Breaks

On my very first day at Stater Brothers' Supermarket as a grocery bagger, the white clerks gave me the nickname 'Troublemaker.' I had no idea why they called me this upon first meeting me, and they said it affectionately and with a warm smile. "Oh, here comes Troublemaker. Good morning! How're you doing? Have you been going around causing trouble?" they asked. I took this greeting in stride. It seemed to be their oblique way of being friendly or at the very least, sociable.

I was the first and only black employee at this particular store in San Bernardino. My being employed here at all in the mid-1960s represented a break in social conventions. The store manager, Basketball Jim, was a tall white man who was a former basketball player at Michigan State University and a rare liberal in this desert area. Hiring a black man had been risky, but he was willing to do it.

Being the only black employee meant that I stuck out like a sore thumb. Gonzalez was Hispanic, the only other minority bagger, and he kept an eye out for me. He was the one who let me know that one particular white bagger was attempting to subjugate and harass me.

Jerry Cheader, was a cheater, so we called him, Jerry Cheater, known for his crafty shortcuts and sneaky habits. Rarely seen working, but always snacking, smoking, or drinking in the stockroom. He was older than I was by two years and had graduated from high school in my older brother's class. He was the oldest of the box-boys at Stater Brothers' and had some "pull" there because his mother was friendly with Basketball Jim. This made him think he could pick on or boss around any of the newer, younger workers and especially any people of color.

Perhaps, he assumed he had power to boss me around. Except I was having none of it.

"Hey, you gotta learn to follow orders I give you," the cheater snapped at me one day when I once again ignored him. "I have seniority over the box boys. I've been here longer. And I don't like you talking 'bout me behind my back."

"Listen to you?" I laughed. "You don't sign my paycheck. You aren't God, and I ain't no dog. But you look stupid and sound even more stupid. If I gotta say anything to you, I say it to your ugly face."

Jerry's face turned red. "Listen boy, you wanna go against me? I'll see you after work.

Then we can settle this. And that punk brother of yours ain't gonna help you. When I get finished with you, even your black momma won't recognize you. You gonna learn to do as you're told."

"We'll see, *boy*! I ain't my brother! You don't know me! But you'll find that out after work. I promise you. I'll be right here waiting."

And that was that. Jerry stalked off, enraged. I went back to work.

Gonzalez sidled up to me. "Aren't you afraid of him?" he asked. "He's gonna try to mess you up, you know? He's got buddies, too!"

"S' okay. I'll be ready for him… or them. And if I gotta die, one or two of them is gonna die too!"

Gonzalez flashed a half-grin at me, assuming I was joking, but when he saw my dead- serious eyes, his widened. "Shit, man. You're crazy!"

"He's not my boss, and I'm no slave," I said firmly. "Taking orders from him will never happen. He's the one who's crazy."

"Well, I gotta hand it to you: you got balls. Cheater really is a jerk. I hate his ass. I just want you to know that if you need any help, I'll back you up. Don't expect that white boy to fight fair, either. He's a nasty, sneaky motherfucker. Don't trust him."

"Hey, it's okay," I said. "You should stay outta this, 'cause it might get ugly. No need for you to get in trouble."

"I guess those old scars on your head mean something," Gonzalez said, his eyes wide in admiration. "Bro, we peoples gotta stick together. We're the only two minority folk here: you, black and me, brown. Don't think my being the only Latino here for years has been easy.

Cheater and I had run-ins before you started. He would sneak up behind me when I was bagging a customer's groceries and kick me in my ankle. Hurt like a motherfucker. We had it out, and I told him my gang of Latinos would fuck his gringo ass up—both him and his family. Never had a problem since. That's one racist sucker. Anyway, I got your back."

After this monologue, Gonzalez went back to the aisle where he was stocking shelves. I rubbed the box-cutter in the pocket of my green store apron.

Toward the end of my shift, I entered the men's locker room to grab the broom. I noticed a small red-and-white Santa Claus decal stuck on the small mirror. Surrounding the mirror on both sides were various graffiti etchings, deep vanilla-colored jagged scratches, and arrow-pierced hearts drawn in red and black ink markers. Some of the older etchings and graffiti had been half-rubbed away or worn down to near invisibility from aging. However, the bold outline of a gothic-styled swastika was sharp and disturbingly clear. Beneath it, silent words shouted mockingly at me: "Hitler Was Right!" I averted my eyes only to see "Niggers and Coons Should Go Back to Africa!" written on the wall in large, blazing black script. These were not the only signs that my presence in the store was not welcomed.

Angry, I left the pleasant coolness of the air-conditioned store, walked out into the blast furnace that was evening in August in San Bernardino, and began to clean up the parking lot. I swept up rubbish like gum and candy wrappers, half-smoked cigarettes hurriedly stepped on, metal soda-bottle caps, and small crushed cartons of strawberry milk before retrieving wayward shopping carts customers had left at the extreme corners of the parking lot.

Beyond the parking lot, the sporadic traffic sounds of humming engines and squealing tires contrasted with racing engines. A few first-time drivers are showing off behind their wheels along the short stretch in front of the store plaza. Inside the supermarket, the hustle and bustle of late shoppers desperate to finish checking out gave rise to a surprise din. This war of sounds was bereft of the usual calm civility that prevailed during shopping lulls. Metal carts crashed and banged against each other. Periodically, products fell from towering stacks with a loud clatter. "Clean-up on aisle eight! Clean-up on aisle eight!" Dolly's voice echoed over the store's loudspeaker.

Outside, my mind was churning over the methods of attack to use against Jerry-the- Cheater. I was looking forward to this clash. His last words had set me on edge. The disrespect he had shown toward me and my family was the straw that broke the camel's back. I was seething inside. It was a familiar, murderous burning, smoldering hotter and hotter. At this point, I didn't care about what I stood to lose from fighting. It was time to put all religious thoughts of piety and forgiveness aside. This was a call to war: black against white.

I steeled my mind to focus on the vital points of Jerry's body and where to direct my attacks. I pictured Jerry's high domed forehead, his lifeless slate-gray eyes, and his weak chin. The half snarl that seemed permanently etched on his arrogant, thin lips made me subconsciously ball my fists. I frowned, thinking about the unconscious way he arrogantly tossed his blond hair back as he shook his head and the way his shifty eyes moved as he talked.

Jerry-the-Cheater drove a vintage tan Volvo, often boasting that it was a gift from his parents. Girls at school were partial to a guy with a car. This fact alone automatically placed him in a class beyond me. Thinking of this only further fueled my hatred.

As I was pushing a string of seven stray shopping carts back to the main parking lot, I saw a familiar car slowly approaching. The quiet automobile crept out of the dark, unlit area of the property. It was Jerry. Apparently, he had clocked out early and wanted to get this thing between us over and done with. When I was close enough to see him behind the wheel, he turned the motor off. Jerry's voice called out in a calm, even tone: "Hey, come over here. Let's talk."

"You wanta talk, get out and come to me. You got anything to say to me, you best stand up and say it like a man," I shot back.

"I just wanta talk. Come here, man."

"I'm not a dog. I don't come when I'm called. You come to me. Don't hide in that stupid- looking car!"

"Don't you think you're being a little ridiculous?"

"You're the one who's ridiculous," I said. "You started this with your stupid attitude. You aren't my boss. You didn't hire me. So get out and see if you can finish what you started."

"Oh, go to hell. I was just trying to apologize, you fucking nigger." With that, he switched the car motor on and angrily gunned it, racing out of the parking lot.

I yelled at the departing car, "Fuck you back, asshole! I'll be waiting whenever you're ready!"

Hours later at home, I felt angry and guilty. I had not acted like a saint. And those words from my mouth had felt weird. But now Jerry-the-Cheater knew my true colors, and I didn't care if he told anyone. I was tired of them all at the store.

But after this, I remain on alert at the store. Walking down the store aisles, rounding blind corners, and entering the vacant, dark stockroom all set me on edge. All are potential combat zones.

I don't see Cheater again and assume the manger or his assistant have deliberately scheduled us to work a different shifts. Still, I remain tense, expecting to see his sly face appear any moment.

About a week later, Gonzalez pulled me aside for a brief chat in the stockroom. "Did you hear what happened? Did you hear the news?" he asked. He looked upset.

"No, what are you talking about?"

"I got my letter. I got drafted. I'm going to 'Nam next month!" "Aww, shit, man! What a bummer!"

"And that's not all. You hear 'bout Jerry?" "No. Now what?"

"Basketball Jim is sending him to clerk school training next week." "You're kidding."

"Nope. I've been here four months longer than him, and he's going to become a clerk before me. This is a serious Union issue now," Gonzalez said. "Told you this was a shitty place to work."

"You got that right," I said, nodding.

Gonzalez turned to walk away, paused, and then shot me a mischievous grin. "By the way, what happened between you and Cheater last week? I heard you guys didn't fight because you called it off. Is that true?"

"Heck no! He wanted to talk, I told him we could talk with our fists, and he drove off," I said. I wasn't surprised to hear that the story had changed.

"You say what?"

"Yep. I was collecting carts out back, and he drove up. Said he wanted to 'talk.' He'd clocked out early. You know him."

"Yeah, I know. He and his buddies rarely actually work. They're always on a smoke-break in the back or pretending to fold boxes. Shit, man. But I heard he said he was kickin' your ass, and you apologized and shit. I couldn't believe it 'cause I know you wanted to kill him," he said.

"Well, I'm still here, and I ain't seen him since that night. He's a fucking asshole liar."

"I told you that. You just watch yourself around here, man. Those whites stick together, you know."

"Okay. Thanks," I said. "Sorry about the draft thing."

"Yeah, well, I gotta get outta here anyway, so I may as well go fight and get paid doing it. But first, I'm going to deal with the manager about the clerk school situation. I may have to sue Shackle Brothers."

Up front, the five cash register stations were running at full speed, their caching bells dinging, the ringing sounds of drawers opening and closing, the clack of numbers being crunched, and the whir of calculator gears grinding making it surprisingly loud. Lines of customers were backed up between the food aisles as the after-work rush brought the usual press of buyers out in droves. The two female clerks, Dolly and Joan, moved like automatons. They both rocked from one foot to the other as they punched in the prices on the register, then shuttled merchandise along the conveyor belt and into the waiting hands of a scrambling bag boy.

Dolly was a no-nonsense worker. When I was paired with her, I had to sack quickly, sometimes frantically endeavoring to keep up with her pace. Still, she could tell when I was getting frustrated and would pause and rock back and forth a few times from one foot to the other while looking back at me. She rarely smiled, and her words were few, but she commanded respect from all of the staff due to her demeanor.

Joan was everyone's favorite because she laughed, goofed off, and joked with workers and customers. Almost everyone who came in contact with her greeted her warmly. Her verbal trademarks consisted of sassy vulgarity and sexual lewdness. If there was ever a pause in the action, Joan would lean forward in a confiding manner and dispense the latest earthy sexual joke she had heard from one of her friends. Both she and Dolly were middle-aged and had worked for the supermarket chain for over fifteen years.

A few days after my exchange with Gonzalez, I was sorting and organizing the greeting card display racks that were in disarray when Joan came over to me.

"Hey, can I ask you something?" her voice dropped to a low whisper. "How come your mother never shops in our store? I've never seen her here. Are you ashamed to ask her to shop where you work? I know you got enough money, 'cause you been working overtime for several weeks now. What's up with that?"

"Come on, Joanie! We can't afford these prices," I said, sighing.

"Whad'ya mean? Look at these coupons in today's paper. We got ground beef and chicken on sale. And we've been running that other special on soups and produce for four days. You aren't gonna tell me you're that hard up for cash. Your father works, doesn't he?"

"Joanie, I can't tell my mother where to shop. She has her own habits. Besides, I'm working all this overtime because I'm saving money for tuition and books. College ain't cheap."

Apparently, she must have thought she'd offended me, because she held her hands up in a placating gesture. "Hey, hey, I'm just jagging with ya. By the way, did you hear the latest about Jerry?"

"No. Should I care?"

"I know you two don't get along, but apparently he and some tramp girl got arrested last night," she said with slightly lowered voice, leaning in like a conspirator.

"You're kidding," I said, my head whipping up and my eyes going wide in surprise.

Glad to have an audience for her gossip, Joan barreled on with her story. "No, God's honest truth. He and some girl were doing the nasty in the back of his car in the parking lot the other night, and the police caught 'em."

"That guy? In that shit-colored thing he calls a car, with some girl, in our lot?"

"Yep. I hear they were doing the '69' with each other, you know what I mean? He's such an ugly guy, too! He always gave me the creeps. I wish he would stay back there in the stockroom all the time. I don't want him walking up behind me. Even though he's young, I wouldn't want him beneath my skirt. Wouldn't let him fuck me for hundred dollars!"

"Joanie! Joanie!" I said, trying to quiet her.

"Oh, making you blush, am I? Sorry kid, you're so holy and all. But that's the news. And his mom and pop were trying to get Basketball Jim to send him to clerical school before this happened. Now with him having an arrest record and all, I guess he's screwed."

"Well, good for him," I said.

"Ha! I knew you'd say that, being so Christian an all. You old hypocrite, you!" Joan laughed.

"Nobody's perfect," I said with a grin.

Joan grinned in return and flicked a damp dust cloth at me. She narrowed her eyes, winked, and motioning with her head for me to come closer. In a lower voice full of confidentiality, she murmured, "You're such a sweet, innocent young man. Tell me... are you still a virgin?

I almost choked. "Joanie, come on!"

She stepped back, laughing. "I'm just jagging with you, silly! Oh my, the look on your face! Anyway, I gotta go outside for a smoke." Joan was still laughing as she walked away, and I hustled off on a pretend errand. I could feel her smile on my departing back. Before leaving,

Joan shouted over to the next register stand where one of the male cashiers and a male bagger idly waited. "Take a lesson from him, boys," she said, nodding in my direction. "You wanna get something done, you gotta know how to have fun... to please!"

"Awww, Joanie! You're just a big tease, you witch!" one laughed. "Cradle-robber!" the other jumped in.

"Nympho-child-molesting witch!"

"I got a magic spell for you, Joanie: my broomstick up your ass tonight!"

Joan enjoyed their name-calling and taunted, "Oh, you think your broomstick can satisfy me? Ha!"

"Hey, you guys watch your mouths. This is a public place, you know," Dolly said.

Eventually, I retreated to the rear of the store. Opening the heavy door to the cold- storage room, I was hit by a frigid blast of refreshing air. This cavern was a place of stark contrasts: despite the cold air, it smelled of souring creams, milks, yogurts, and a selection of juices. Several items were open, a number of employees secretly sampled items throughout the week. These interlopers rarely finished the goods they opened, and they were later found stale, sour, and flat.

Basketball Jim had enough on his hands as it was, and he overlooked these petty thefts by his employees. Union reps were bothering him about needing more minority representation in the workforce as a result of a new policy called 'Affirmative Action.' White gang leaders had started hanging around, harassing customers. Some bullies had threatened the entire store's staff. There were bolder shoplifting attempts. And now, he had to deal with the fallout from Jerry-the-Cheater getting arrested.

I soon left this job behind to concentrate on my studies and was relieved to do so. I would concentrate my efforts to graduate from community college. After this I could launch I took a small step backward. My legs felt wobbly. Coach Matlah's bald dome, bright red face, sun-burned neck, and large cauliflower ears filled my vision. His glowering stare was filled with intense hate. Fiery daggers shot from his eyes. Not giving me a chance to say anything, he continued shouting, his voice taking on a wild tone. "That son of a bitch nigger must be crazy! I'll rip his fucking head off!" I knew then and there that I must intensify my search for a university speech scholarship far from home. The life of an athlete for me was a dead end. To remain there was unhealthy.

CHAPTER 10

Reality Checks

I took a small step backward. My legs felt wobbly. Matlah's sun blistered bald dome, crimson face, burned red neck, and large cauliflower ears filled my vision. His stare glowered He continued shouting like a mad man, his voice taking on a wild tone. "That son of a bitch nigger must be crazy! I'll rip his fucking head off!"

Coach Matlah, was the wrestling coach and a gym teacher at San Bernardino Valley College, seemed like a friend to everybody. At least this was his surface appearance. All the first-year white boys routinely greeted Coach Matlah by his first name as they filed into and out of the locker room, and he always returned their salutations with smiles and friendly banter.

One morning during my second year at San Bernardino Valley College, I made the mistake of assuming that, having been on the wrestling team with him and worked out with him, I could treat him the same way the white students did.

As we were filing out of the locker room after our badminton class, I called out to him exactly the way the other white boys always had: "Good morning, Bill. How're you today?"

Suddenly, as if air had been sucked out of the room, there was an uncomfortable silence. Then he exploded. Coach Bill Matlah charged toward me like a raging bull. In that moment, my mind's eye replaced his figure with that of the mean White man who had terrorized me when I was younger. He was that boogeyman who had chased me off a high school football field years earlier. The difference was that I was no longer small, scared child. I was not going to run. As the coach closed in he shouted at me, "What did you say? Are you talking to me? Who the hell do you think you are, you little black Sambo? Say what you just said to me again!"

My legs were frozen. I had not moved from my locker. Luckily for me, several arms grabbed him and held him back, but he continued to rant and struggle, cursing me as if I had committed a horrible crime. It took him a while to quiet down.

Still in shock, I had not moved. My feet seemed rooted into the cement floor. Coach Matlah and I had always gotten along well. He had never shown any hint of dislike for me. Younger white boys who were my peers routinely addressed him as "Bill." I thought I had been respectful with my greeting. So what had I done wrong?

Immediately, two other coaches hurried to the scene and dragged the raving teacher away, I heard a warning voice nearby. A Hispanic classmate was changing near my locker.

"Hey man, you'd better leave. You disrespected him. First name? You crazy! Don't you know where he's from?"

The trembling, urgency in his voice finally broke me out of my trance. He repeated his advice. "Man, you better hurry up and leave. They still trying to hold him back. Vamoose, man!"

I glanced over at two black classmates on benches further away. They were not in my class, but they were silent raising their eyebrows at me. I could tell they thought I was crazy to still be in the locker room. Sounds of panic are everywhere.

Coach Matlah was still shouting, "That little nigger! Who does he think he is? I'm gonna break his neck! You hear me! Let go me!"

"Calm down, calm down," the track coach said. "He meant no harm. You know that." "Who the hell does that little fool think he is? Lemme go! The fucking twerp!" "Come on, calm down. He meant no harm. Watch your language, man."

The two other coaches were clearly struggling to control the raging human bull that had gone berserk. The atmosphere was thick with fear and hate. It was hard to breath, and my chest suddenly felt heavy.

The track coach caught my eyes and, stern-faced, jerked his head rapidly toward the exit. Coming to my senses, I finally realized it wasn't wise to stick around. I didn't want to run or lose face, so I carefully and deliberately walked out of the building. By the time I made it outside, I was shaking all over. My hands had gone, and my head buzzed as if I had been drugged.

It would be several days before I could muster the courage to return to my gym locker. I never saw Coach Matlah again. I had already been considering whether to return to the track and wrestling teams this year, and now my decision was made for me. There is no way I would be returning.

However, a few week later, Coach Vargas, a Hispanic track coach at my school, attempted to convince me to rethink my decision: "We want you to come back. You know, if you don't run for this school, you're throwing away your future. How are you going to get a university education? You know your parents can't afford to pay high tuition bills. Track is your ticket. Think, man. "

"I'll think about it, "I allowed, "but I'm really not comfortable here anymore."

"Oh, forget about Bill Matlah," he said, waving his hand in the air as though waving away a fly. "He's from Alabama. You should'a known old habits die hard. Forget about it. It's no big deal. I guarantee you there will be a scholarship waiting for you at Redlands University if you run for us this next season. Don't throw your ticket away. Think, man. Life is short. Don't do something you'll regret."

"Okay. Thanks, coach. I gotta go," I said, cutting our interview short.

I had lettered running track in both high school and college. Bring trophies home to my mother was my oblique way of showing her that despite her doubts about my health I could successfully compete. I knew my parents really did not approve of these energies spent on non-godly ventures. There were many days and weeks of fasting without food that undoubtedly affected my performances. I always felt to be underachieving. Despite my promise to Coach Vargas to "think about it," I knew this was the end of SBVC sports for me. This was not the first time, nor would it be the last, that I was called the N-word by an authority figure, but I was shocked that this offense came from a teacher. Besides, we lived in California, not the dreaded South.

I resented being told that the only way to further my education was through sports. I bristled at the notion that the only areas where Black Americans could excel were in sports, singing, or dancing. I knew I had other skills.

Even as things had turned sour with the track team, I was travelling around the state with the speech and debate team. On one trip to the campus of USC in Los Angeles, my new debate partner and I decided to do something crazy. USC student athlete O.J. Simpson had recently won the NCAA Heisman Trophy, and his image was everywhere on television ads and billboards. My partner and I decided to walk around the empty campus buildings on a quiet Saturday afternoon, yelling like idiots.

"Yo! O.J.! Where are you?"

"Come on out, O.J.! Come out, come out wherever you are!" "O.J.! O.J.! O.J.!"

It's surprising we weren't approached by campus security.

After this small feat of ours—challenging O.J. Simpson—we felt especially proud of ourselves. So, of course, shortly after that, we were struggling to find the men's lavatory.

Everyplace marked "Toilet" was locked, and we needed to use the restroom before our next ninety-minute debate round. Eventually, we located an unlocked restroom close to our assigned debate room. As we were leaving, two neatly dressed girls entered. We all stared at each other first in shock, and then in embarrassment. The girls covered their mouths and screamed, "What are you doing in here? This is the ladies' room!"

We rushed out, flustered by our dumb mistake. Even worse, those same girls entered our debate room just minutes later. They were our competitors from another school. We ended up losing this debate round, still completely flustered and embarrassed. It was worse than if campus security had detained us.

At other tournaments, I also competed in the short Oral Interpretation of Literature events, and I particularly enjoyed putting together poetry and short story programs for these events. I earn many honors performing the works of Langston Hughes, Countee Cullen, James Baldwin, Maya Angelou, Gwendolyn Brooks, and other black American writers.

As a student at San Bernardino high school, I had my original poetry published in the *Scriptorian* literary magazine. However, on the competitive speech circuit it became clear that works by acclaimed black writers focusing on racial intolerance did not appeal to judges. This may have been due to the fact that all of my judges had been white. I suspected that they had limited interest in ethnic protest literature. I never once had any judges of color for competitive speech events. My first formal speech teacher at college claimed that I only thought about skin color. Her assumption was far from accurate, so I set out to prove that I could focus on non race related topics.

Entering Expository Speech competition I had a chance. My speech for this event was about ESP, or extra-sensory perception. I became California's state junior college co-champion in the event. This honor helped earn my speech scholarship to Nebraska Wesleyan University, becoming the only black male in the senior class. During my time there, I became the president of our chapter of national Phi Rho Psi speech fraternity. I was carrying on our family's pioneering tradition.

I also became the captain of our debate squad, and we travelled around the country. I became the Nebraska state champion in

Persuasive Speaking, and also finalist in the Extemporaneous Speaking event. I was event finalist in the National Interstate Oratorical Contest held in Detroit, where my competition topic was "Violent Communication."

Another highlight at this College was the first time meeting an important Black man.

One of my first public interactions with a bone fide rule breaker was with African-American journalist Louis Lomax. In 1968, the nation was in turmoil following Dr. King's recent assassination. At the time, I was the Men's student body president at San Bernardino Valley College, and I was assigned to interview this guest at our school on a televised college program. Learning that Mr. Lomax was the author of _The Negro Revolt_ only added to my nervous excitement.

Mr. Lomax turned out to be articulate, well groomed, and competent. He did not rant and rave like most of the black ministers I had grown up observing. He was well-researched and well-read in his arguments and well-travelled internationally. His communication skills were remarkable, and he presented a compelling portrait of an America with many sides, faces, and unfulfilled promises to its citizens. During our interview, he said to me, "America is like an A+ student who is committed to only getting "D" grades."

I wanted to do my part to change this and began considering a career as a lawyer or an elected official. These ambitions brought an unexpected change in my life's direction. This would involve personal relationships and vocational engagements.

CHAPTER 11

The Gingerbread House

[1962] **Our family lived in a shack at the edge of San Bernardino for five years.** Both our church and the shack on Waterman Avenue were close to Interstate 95. Shack life was a new experience: there was an outdoor toilet and a metal washtub for outside bathing. These were especially demeaning for us older kids, because we had experienced a far more comfortable life. Even more embarrassing was listening to my dad preach to members of our congregation about a better life to come in Heaven when their basic standard of living was significantly higher than ours. They probably thought we were crazy, and I had to agree. Despite escaping the eye-burning L.A. smog, I was miserable in "the sticks." This new social embarrassment only added to my feeling of living on the social fringes.

The house was a patchwork of untidiness, disrepair, and outright shabbiness. We needed to place buckets and emergency cooking pots on the ground to catch rain water that leaked in. The kitchen, hallway, and bathroom all let water in like a sieve. The indoor toilet was unusable due to severe plumbing problems. Half of the house leaned to the side. I patched cracks between window and door frames with rags and paper to keep the winter winds out. I became expert at using masking tape. Most of the rotten floorboards creaked and bounced like an aged trampoline. The living room carpet was threadbare. There were no pictures on any of the walls, just drab wallpaper everywhere. All fifteen of us live in this cramped, stuffy, dark, moldy shell like crabs.

We prayed daily, "The Lord is my shepherd, I shall not want," but we had many, many wants. Us kids simply tried to pretend we had the things we desperately needed: warm, dry rooms, plentiful food, and social respect. To our parents, these were trivial things. Life was better when you were making sacrifices and being without. This was a kind of mind control that our parents deemed "The will of the God." Our situation and station in life would only change if God wanted it to change. To take matters into our own hands and control our own destiny would be sinful and seen as acts of disbelief. Our parents wanted us to become miniature Jesuses. I wanted to be myself.

Years before we actually moved out to San Bernardino, I had a crush on on the eldest Elmwood girl at our church out there. B.B. was ten or twelve years older than me, but she was so small in stature that we kids took her to be one of us. Her smooth chocolate skin, attractive features, pleasant smile from pouty lips, short movie-star hairstyle, and naturally long eyelashes made her beautiful. However, the voice coming from her tiny body was squeaky, and she had a slight speech impediment. These attributes made B.B. seem like a life-sized doll to us kids, and she was someone I could turn to for hugs. Yet her perfect appearance only hinted at her adult professionalism. Soon, she graduated from the local community college and became a court reporter, a successful, professional woman. I thought myself in love with B.B.

One weekend, my heart was broken by an announcement. B.B. Elmwood was getting married to Titus Fletcher, a stranger who had visited our church only once. He was a handsome military man from Ohio with smooth almond-colored skin. He obviously knew how to charm B.B., and he drove a late-model car. I didn't even have a bicycle.

After B.B.'s marriage, the Elmwood family moved away, and the saints seemed relieved. However, the Elmwood's had been living in the gingerbread-colored shack owned by the church, and after some thieves broke in, it became apparent that a human alarm system was needed. Our father, now the church pastor, recruited a dark-skinned, oily-faced bald man named Murray to live there. His bulging belly hung sloppily over baggy pants that perennially revealed a plumber's crack. I figured he was from skid row and that dad was doing charity work. Slow Belly Murphy, as us kids called him, had bulging reddish eyes and a grotesque mouth with just two or three long, yellow-brown teeth poking from black gums. He revealed these whenever he emitted a gurgling laugh, which happened after every other word he spoke. He coughed a lot and spit out thick, nasty phlegm. Slow Belly Murphy lurched when he walked and always looked like he was on the verge of toppling over. His thick, gnarled fingers were like large rusty bolts, and he used them to sneakily eat snack while sitting in the rear of the church. The sight of Slow Belly Murphy was both scary and entertaining.

Slow Belly Murphy lived in the gingerbread shack house rent-free as the church grounds watchman before we moved from L.A. to San Bernardino and replaced him. During church services, he always sat at the rear of the church, watching, but never participating. Sometimes, after worship services, he would offer thick wedges of gingerbread to the church attendees.

Some reluctantly accepted his generosity. To us kids, hungry after the long sermons, the spicy scent of fresh ginger cake was tempting.

However, our mother kept an eye on us after church services whenever Slow Belly was around, and we were strictly forbidden from accepting food from others without permission. No matter how persistent the person was or how enticing the food looked, we had to refuse. "You never know what he puts in that stuff," mom said. "That man is not to be trusted."

Some folk in our church claimed that Slow Belly smelled like booze from hitting the bottle frequently, that he was a worker of Satan, and that he was not to be trusted. Adding to this belief was the fact that a mysterious, frail, dark woman had been seen visiting his house under the pretense of bringing him food.

Needless to say, we were all surprised when he did not show up after church for several days in a row. When people started asking around, it was discovered that the perimeter property lights had not been turned on for three nights running. My father went to the house to investigate, and he immediately called an ambulance and the police. Slow Belly Murphy had been dead for several days. Dad said the smell inside the house was horrific, adding, "It's a shame Brother Murphy died alone."

The officials investigating the case announced that old Slow Belly had been sick and died of natural causes. My parents considered burning the house down. We thought a ghost resided in it. One of the adult male church members said that the body had bloated and burst open, igniting my imagination is an image of Slow Belly's huge, bulging stomach exploding everywhere. For several months, only adults were permitted inside. Dad's command was clear:

"Stay away from there, you hear me?" This was fine with me, as I stayed as far from that brown house as possible. I was afraid that blood and other body parts might still be hanging from the ceiling. And then there might be that awful smell of death. I had been to enough funerals to know that large floral arrangements do not mask that distinctive smell.

So when our entire family of fifteen moved into that dilapidated shack just a few months later, I was equal parts bewildered and traumatized.

When our father made this announcement, he claimed that the Lord had been "dealing with" him. Of course, this announcement came after another one of his long fasts. We would leave our comfortable four-bedroom house on the west side and live in the brown shack in the desert. There would be no discussion or vote on the matter because the Lord had been clear about this. After all, this was the same voice that had told him to marry our mother. Dad assured us that there was nothing to be afraid of about living in that house.

Dad again claimed that the voice of God speaking to him. We had no choice but to believe that our father was holy and very special. No one else we knew ever made such claims. Only important figures in the Bible had such abilities.

He claimed that this move was a "test" like the one God had given to Job in the Bible.

This sounded pretty bleak to me. Job had to lose everything before his situation changed. I didn't want that for us. And yet, it happened anyway. Our father gave up his well-paying job working for the county to start his own contracting business when we moved out to San Bernardino. Later, he felt moved by the Holy Spirit to become church elder and then a full-time pastor, eventually quitting the electrical business altogether. He said, "You just must believe and be like Jesus. Only then will you be saved! Don't be like those people who laughed at Noah and his Ark. They died terrible deaths."

CHAPTER 12

Toward Liberation

We drove in silence for a while. Excitement had only slightly ebbed from exhaustion. The ocean view from Highway 101 had soothed the past month of emotional events. We were newlyweds pulling away from the chains in the desert starting a new life. Anywhere away from this dry pit would be better. Vassar Jean, my first bride had the same resolve. I called her "VJ". Her father had named her this because he had been in the Navy when victory over Japan had been achieved. Now, all we needed to do was collect her belongings in the San Francisco State University dorm. We would be heading to Illinois where I had would complete my master's degree. I just was worried about how many additional items we would be hauling. Ours would be a long cross-country marathon. There was no telling what lay ahead. I quizzed VJ about the future load we would pick up.

"Are you sure we have enough room for your things still on campus?" Vassar assured me there was no need to get uptight. I would learn to appreciate that she was not a clothes addict or shop-a-holic.

"Don't worry so much" she said laughing, "I'm just a student, too, you know. Just a few clothes and books. Things like hot-plate, coffee pot, and plants won't take that much room. I can give other stuff away." I was relieved hearing this. If we had to pull more heavy weight up and down mountains, there might be other issues besides increased gasoline costs. I was depending on three credit cards already close to max.

"Sounds like a plan," I replied, "We'll see. Just hope we don't need to rent a U-haul." Vassar's assurances calmed my impatience and anxiety.

"Are you kidding! Listen, I don't have that much stuff. Trust me. It's going to work out. Let's just take our time and be safe." I began to feel we were really going to make this thing work.

"Okay. Thanks. After Frisco we'll hit Nebraska. Some poet friends have offered us a place to stay before Illinois."

"Wow, that's great! Well take your time. Let's keep an eye on the speed-Iimit and try to be patient. We can't afford any speeding tickets. Okay? I know you're worried about Grad school, but you do have at least a week before classes start." Vassar smiled and I relaxed at the thought that soon we'd be comfortable, snuggling into one another in a wash of guiltless wedded bliss.

Pressing the car accelerator firmer, the speedometer needle inched ten miles above the speed limit. The scenery flew by faster. Every second we moved further away from that church, the brown gingerbread house, the thirsty desert of shame, and judgmental decrees, I relaxed.

Whatever we did, we or I could embrace the ownership of our acts. I exhaled and relaxed, easing into the new adventure. I was officially no longer a fringe member of the True Believers. This brought a huge feeling of relief.

*****

Flashback. We were dancing in the behind the brown lopsided shack, beneath a blazing hot California desert. My mother's grip on my wrists was surprising strong. I could not shake free but kept an eye on the house. At any moment dad could quickly come outside to join our heated discussion. If he did come out there was no telling how things would escalate. My unwilling dance partner was trying to keep me from following through with my crazy marriage announcement. Mom made valiant arguments to persuade against becoming an official family outcast. I believed I was doing the right thing. Now I was hearing her accusations.

"You have really changed. Look at you! And listen to you! Marry a Catholic? And a dark one at that! Don't you know that we love you?" I could tell by her grip that she was concerned. But I did not want to beat around the bush. My words were short. No long debate. The sun was too hot in the yard.

"Mom, I've got to go my way. Stand on my own. This is my life you know." We held each other's forearms. My mother and I were practically dancing in a slow circle outside our house. Trying to keep the bright sun out of our own eyes. The odd backyard scene may have looked comical to observers. We were being scorched under a typical blazing San Bernardino sun. Both of us deadly serious. The evening before I had introduced my fiancée, VJ, to meet my parents. I announced that we would be getting married.

I had casually known VJ from a distance as a high school freshman. She had been a senior in my older brother's class. Years later, after dropping out of Seminary in Indiana, we had met at the Mill School Day Care Center. There she held a summer job as a preschool teacher. For a few years VJ had worked with several of my younger sibling. After High School graduation she had enrolled in San Francisco University, returning to her job during summers. She had first- hand experiences witnessing the shocking social behaviors of my youngest siblings. That summer we dated a few times and hit it off. A memorable date was when we drove to Los Angeles to hear Dionne Warwick sing in the Greek Theater. After that date I was ready to convince Vassar to hitch her wagon to my star. I asked her to marry me. She said yes.

Days later, my mother and I had stood alone in the yard far from the shambles of our house. Privacy was our hope. There would be no interruptions, prying eyes or listening ears. Mom was grilling me in the yard out of earshot of dad. I was afraid that any minute he would come outside and start preaching again. His theme predictably would be that we as a family had been chosen to suffer for Jesus. He saw himself in some kind of biblical role.

Ancient like Noah and the Ark. Or longsuffering Job. The San Bernardino desert was the place dad claimed God had placed him. To accept this notion would keep me permanently imprisoned in a ridiculous religious box. I was increasingly ashamed to be associated with "Holy Rollers" and fundamentalism. I had to break away once and for all. Simply leaving home for school had not been enough. My eyes and mind had become open to realities, contradictions, and futility.

Mom continued to argue. "You know your father has a reputation in this town. If you were so set on marriage outside of our group, you should have told me." I did not want to stand long in the sun arguing. I recognized the pointlessness of arguing. And I was not going to go over tired worn out issues arguing with my mother. After years on observation and reflecting my mind was made up. I stuck to my guns.

"Mom, I already know what you and dad think about my marriage. I just thought it civil to introduce you to my future wife. Don't worry, we will be moving away immediately after the ceremony. We will not be living here to embarrass you."

My mother had that familiar evangelist's intense look in her eyes. Worry lines creased her eyes face. Her voice trembled with the usual edge of fear. She blurted out another torrent of bible verses warning doom. Hell, fire and brimstone from the sky and the lake of fire to be feared.

Eternal damnation. Her voice and tone reflected a well practice routine prophesying the end of the world. She shook my arms as her words spilled out. Next, I noticed a different persuasive tact. Her voice softened and volume lowered.

"Listen, Honey! LISTEN to me! This is all happening too fast. Just too soon! You should WAIT! We love you! I told you there was a young Philippine girl at Loma Linda Hospital I want you to meet. She's a nurse. Why don't you wait and meet her? Think of your father's reputation." Those last few words came out like a harsh whisper.

Mom stared with fierce intensity into my eyes as if to bore a hole in my head. I stared back. No more words. We were going to settle this, and I was not going to be moved. Slowly, after several of minutes of silence her grip on my forearms loosen. The look in her eyes were of resignation. "You've changed", she said with a sigh, her voice dropped lower. "I know the devil must be using you, but how can you do this to your father?" I was silent. Living my life to please others was no longer in the cards. This was the last time we spoke. I was no longer welcome to enter the place called home again.

Days before that backyard confrontation, upon learning that Vassar's religious background was Catholic, dad had preached about the theological errors of Catholicism. He was emphatic that VJ become a Pentecostal. An induction into the dreadful world of fundamentalist thinking. I adamantly opposed this. I viewed our pending marriage as a clear breaking away from closed minded theologies.

I did not say it, but dad's reputation was the last thing I cared about. I needed to break away clear and final. My folks viewed our marriage as a threat. A symbolic thumbing my nose at their fundamental Christian principles. I did not care. I simply wanted to take control of my own destiny. I was tired of being led by the nose-ring by ancient scriptures, and conflicting bible interpretations. This way of life usually changed on the whims of uneducated, narrow-minded leadership. Decrees that changed depending size of church congregation or the minister's skill at persuasion. In my view, organized religious was a messed-up game. A slick business for connivers.

Most ministers in our sect preached: "No beards or facial hair allowed!" Others forbid the wearing of bushy Afro hairstyles. Women might be frowned upon if they dared wear Moo- Moos, or Sack dresses. These were fashionable style rages at the time. There had long been a policy split over adornments like wearing earrings or necklaces. This was East coast versus West coast ideologies. However, regardless the region, a woman was guaranteed a place in Hell if caught in above knee skirts or red lips. Most damning to me was the undeniable racist beliefs and behaviors. Blacks were encouraged to worship only with Blacks, Whites with Whites. These were holy folk. They called themselves "Saints". That I dared entertain marrying a Catholic girl was certain damnation. My mother reiterated the church party-line. Idol worshippers. Heretics. Words my father had routinely preached. Her words were louder with more intensity.

"Honey! Honey! Don't let the devil use you. You must not turn your back on god's words. Let me find a suitable girl for you!" My pride made me quickly rebuff what I perceived an insult using a bit of sarcasm.

"Thanks mom, but I don't need you to fix-me-up with anyone. I know what I like and what I want. God tells you and dad this and that. Your life is stuck in the dark ages. But I do not want to live in a life like this!"

I spoke these words jerking my head toward the shambles of the crumbling house behind me. My eyes swept the junk and weeds, the utter desolation. Despair surrounded us. We had come a long way from the comforts of Crocker Street in Los Angeles. I tried to pry my mom's hands loose from gripping me. But she held firm. Pleading.

"Dear! Dear... how can you do this to your father? We love you...Suffering for Christ is the will of God...how can you say we are brainwashed. The Holy Bible is...." I cut her off not wanting to hear the broken record on rewind. There was nothing to be negotiated. I was getting married and leaving. My voice rose almost shouting.

"Mom! Doesn't the bible say people should freely come by choice? All these years I have been loyal to your and dad! I love you both, but I've got to live my own life without being forced into a certain way! Not yours! This is my happiness. All I'm asking is that you come to our wedding. You, dad, the whole family are invited. Haven't you always said, as long as I do what makes me happy, you'll be happy?

She was silent and did not answer. And I did not want to say anymore. I could not tell her that choosing to live a double life on the social fringes sickened me. I no longer felt the need to pretend that I enjoyed compulsory faith that had been forced upon me before I was even five years of age. This fringe lifestyle of being manipulated and controlled had to cease.

Slowly I pried my mother's warm worn fingers off my arms and pulled away. I could see in her eyes not tears, but a frantic look of desperation. Like I had been her life raft slipping away.

Fading hope. Mom seemed to withdraw into a shell. I was lost to her, to them. This would mark an end to going around and around in a merry-go-round of words. I had tired of hearing platitudes about a thing called "love". No more spinning like children on a playground merry- go-round. I would at last be free to be me.

CHAPTER 13

Things Left Behind

"There's something I want you to do", he said with **an air of gravity.** Dad and I stood face to face in the old gingerbread shack. I could tell by the gravity of his voice that this was a matter of importance. I also knew without looking his eyes had that stern fiery look this was serious business. My stomach knotted up and the old familiar lump in my throat was back. One did not ask questions. Averting my eyes, I glance around the brown shack we called our home, and patiently waited for his next words. As they slowly registered in my mind, I knew it was what he called the Lord's business. This was to be considered a holy matter. His vocal tone bordered on secret urgency. It was a command wrapped in the guise of a conspiratorial request. This was new. Dad's words shocked me.

"I want you to go down to the church. There's a young White guy there who is trying to hide from the police. I can't have that. He says that because he is Homosexual they have been harassing him. He's on the run. He wants asylum in our church. I don't want us to get mixed up in this. You talk to him. He cannot stay, because this is a holy place. I'm depending on you. See what you can do."

I nodded my head and without a word left the house. I was dad's soldier robot. I was supposed to expel the stranger from our church. Tradition held that anyone could find refuge in a church. Deep inside my heart I felt disappointed because dad had sent me to do his dirty work. At the back of our lot stood the white church, a painted stucco rectangular building in which we worshipped.

It looked like a small, low, plain box bunker despite the crude fluorescent lights affixed to two-by-four wooden beams shaped like a cross. This crucifix was centered at the crown of structure's roof. Large black block letters painted across the face of the white building announced our holy roller denomination: BETHEL APOSTOLIC FAITH. Our group was clear competition with the large pink, cavernous structure in the next lot. The competing church was on an adjourning parcel of land close the street. Their congregation no doubt heard louder street rumbles than we did. Sixteen and eighteen wheelers taking the local business route off I-95 enjoyed to free flow of Waterman Avenue. Two small symbolic crosses on both sides of the double-door entry church doors were eye catchers. A small electric sign box sealed with glass announced this was the CHURCH OF GOD IN CHRIST. Our competitors. Their paved parking lot was only full twice a week. In contrast, our church doors were open for business six days weekly. However, our visitors were rare.

Slowly walking to the back of the lot to our church edifice, my shoes made crunching sounds on the ground. An Air Force F-1 fighter plane suddenly roared low overhead. Engines throttling down were aimed for the Norton Air Base runway. My ears experienced a ringing sound. After a moment I could hear my footsteps in the gravel again. This was our parking lot, unpaved, also a dust bowl. When cars the saints drove turned off Waterman Avenue, barely reducing car speed, their wheels churned up gravel, sand, and dust that took a while to settle. People, who knew this factor waited in their cars a minute or two before exiting. The unlucky ones caught walking toward the small prison-like structure of BETHEL, would feel the effects of fallout from new rolling arrivals. Hands cupped over mouths, or handkerchiefs became sudden shields until the dusty debris settled. Dust would be on brows, seep and sifting into once clean fashion finery. This stormy wake did not generate warm feelings toward offending arrivals.

At the church doorway I stomped my feet a few times on the asphalt pad before entering. Pushing the wooden door open the tight iron spring resistance responded with expected stubbornness. Wedging my shoulder against the door ensured that the door would not spring back before I was completely inside. The church was semi dark. No lights were on even though it was daytime. I squinted my eyes searching for the stranger whom my father said would be waiting for an answer. Ambient light from the row of three narrow windows located high on both sides of the building provided staggered relief from natural shadows. The young guy was huddled in a dark corner. He was shaking from head to toe. His face was drained and pale. He pressed his lips so tight that it was obvious even his teeth were clinched. As I moved closer the fright in his eyes made me feel sorry for his situation. My mind was immediately in turmoil as to what I was going to say or do. I had not given this any thought before entering the building. Having responded to my father like a trained robot, now I was in a fix. What exactly did my father expect me to say? I was in a quandary how to justify kicking this frightened soul out of the building we often called our sanctuary.

Maybe I should get some situation, I thought to myself. I needed a better picture of this fellow's situation. I would be direct, but I wanted to first put this person more at ease. Using a friendly voice made my opening as friendly and non-judgmental as possible.

"Ah, there you are. It's a little cold in here. Are you okay? What's up?" The fright in his eyes now became more pronounced as his voice squeaked shakily in reply. He was terrified. The roar of another low approaching F-1 fighter heading to Norton did not help. His figure seemed to shrink deeper into the corner he occupied. He spoke.

"Please…You … you…gotta help me! They're tr…tr…try… trying get me! Your bro…brother, Johan, said I should c…c… co…come here if ever I needed help. Can you help me? My name is Ken."

The pale ragged look beneath the long unkept blonde hair, rumpled T-shirt, and smelly jeans, supported a tale of playing hide and seek during the night. He was on the run. This asylum seeker had spent the past evening one step ahead of San Bernardino law enforcement. Those cops had and reputation of being brutes. A wild party had been broken up, people attacked and taken to the station. Ken had been one of the lucky few escaping arrest. But I needed more information.

"Why are the police after you?" Making my voice sound non-accusative I probed. His reply did not surprise me.

"Honestly, I did nothing wrong. But I have a bad relationship with police here. They have accosted me before and it did not go well. I was slapped around and punched just because I am against the war, and for free love. You know they hate all of us longhairs. I'm called Hippie-Faggot all the time. I'm afraid if they catch me this time something worse will happen to me. Nobody would know. I have no family to run to. Please, don't let them catch me."

In the back of my mind flashed the thought of in our church we professed that God was love. We routinely sang about having the love of Jesus in our hearts. This was one of the most popular songs when singing we jumped for joy. But I had my orders from dad. This White fugitive was not to be allowed to stay hidden. The tightness in my throat had become a dull ache. I had heard and seen my father demonstrate his values about Gay people. My older brother, Johan, had already been expelled from our family due to his open sexual orientation. To me, refusing to provide shelter conflicted with my understanding of what churches generally, historically, represented. Dad had left it for me to do the dirty work. I was to be the spiritual assassin. Suddenly, it seemed as if the walls of this small sanctuary closed in on me.

The church felt like an ice box. My throat tightened and I was on the verge of choking. Stifling this environment became. I wanted to exit the building as soon as possible. I was desperate to get past this conflict. We were supposed to be representative of God's love. Somehow, I needed to show our compassion. Trying to make my words sound convincing I leveled with the frantic stranger.

"Listen, I know you're in a tight spot. I know you think our church can solve your problem. But, I should tell you ours is a different type church. Our preacher believes the bible is against Gays. He also is not comfortable with any appearance of aiding and abetting. Our church is extremely old fashion. In the end, our pastor will side with the police. He is strictly old school."

By the anguish look mixed with terror on the young man's face, my words had been a huge shock. His voice and behavior confirmed.

"Oh My God! Then what am I supposed to do? Oh my God! Oh-hhh My God!!!"

He squirmed like a bug stuck on a mounting pin. Tears welled in his eyes spilling down his face. He hid his wet face with his arms and sobbed as his entire frame shook. The trembling stage had ended. Watching the effect of my honesty made me feel pangs of guilt. I had told him what I knew of our reality. This was not, nor could be his safe harbor. Our church was not a place of unpretentious warmth and acceptance. There were strings, edits, and restrictions. Our God was a jealous, punitive, and demanding.

The young man's sobbing grew louder, his repeated question challenged me. "W-w-what can I do? What can I do? I...I..I ... need help!"

I tried my best to soften the blows of reality. "Well, all I can say is, stay here and pray as long as you like. But maybe in an hour or so you should leave. I don't think it's a good idea to let my father find you still here when comes back later this evening. He'll probably call the cops and turn you in."

The youth raised his head and uncovered his teary eyes. "You think that will work? I really can't let those pigs take me in again."

"Well, I'm not going to tell anyone where you are. My lips are sealed. But, I cannot guarantee when my father is coming back inside this edifice. However, you're taking a big risk if you're here over two hours and he finds out. That's all I can say."

Immediate relief spread over the young man's visage. He gushed with relief. "Oh Thank you! Thank You! I'll be gone by then. I promise you. No worry. Thank you so much! I really appreciate any help you guys can give. Thank you! Thank you! Thank you! God bless you!"

I felt it had been cowardly on my dad's part to delegate this decision to me. I was not the church leader. Also, I felt bad to have suggested the fugitive should pray inside BETHEL. This was one ritual that for years had, to me more than symbolized torture. I hated that praying part. Kneeling for long extended time periods on the cold gray concrete floor was no comfort place. Closer to the pulpit and preaching area was a threadbare carpet. Only if one knelt at an obtuse angle could my knees find the sparse floor cover. Wedging elbows and rest one's body into jig-saw formations on the dark, smelly, pressed wood chairs all locked in a parade of five, could become sadistic exercises. I hated the smell of old oiled wood. The sharp seat edges, the…. Numbness in arm and leg joints, routinely following by lightheaded dizziness after long periods of prayer. It took me creating mind games and various goal-setting time periods to adjust to rituals in this building. This was a place of expected spiritual marathons.

I had no idea how long the stranger would last in hiding. Anxiety began to build in the pit of my stomach. And remaining inside BETHEL was neither physically nor psychologically comfortable. Maybe we saints had been kidding ourselves calling "the-little-white-church-in-the-valley" our refuge from the world. We looked forward to the warmth produced by our body heat, lusty exuberant singing, furious hand clapping, thunderous foot stomping. Our spirited jumping and shouting were factors producing the charm we called God's love. Ours was a togetherness that took a lot of hutzpah for strangers to overcome curiosity just to venture inside. Also, there was lust. One could say this was a human fundamental. We were rapidly entering the ripe age for experimentations and explorations. We were vulnerable.

*****

FLASHBACK – There were two rows of limp bodies were kneeling, stomachs pressing against a wooden row of attached seats. My siblings and I were under orders. Dry tear tracks etched down faces from this torture. Three of my young brothers had their arms lifted palms open toward the ceiling. They were loyal soldiers. On the other hand, the five girls, my sisters, had slumped down to resting on their hips. Two still postured with their arms half raised like victims in a holdup. Another two braced their heads with single arms bent behind the head, hand clutching the elbow of the other arm still straight held firmly against an ear. The last girl was resting her head on the seat in deep slumber. Droning voices of those awake were saying "Thank You Jesus" in unison like a damaged recording loop. These elements were buffered by the loud groaning air conditioner pushing soothing coolness. The atmosphere of dread was punctuated by distant sounds of firecrackers and gunshots outside. This practice went on for several years.

Our rituals of active worship momentarily had the effect of keeping our father at bay. He was the punisher. The arm of God. With a slim wooden switch from a tree branch in hand he sat on the pulpit in a large thronelike dark oak chair. His head leaned against the wall. Eyes closed.

Dad was formally the Pentecostal church pastor. But to me he was God, or the prison warden. He made no bones about making sure that we worshipped in the proper way. To arm ourselves, he said, against the world. He justified this regimen quoting scriptures: "As for me and my house, we will serve the lord!" By the time our family moved to San Bernardino, we all recognized dad as the Lord's enforcer.

Friday nights were not a weekend I looked forward to. It was a day marking weeks, months, and years designated for praying. Longer times spent praying. For one hour or more my brothers and sisters would be forced to stay kneeling on the concrete floor with our arms uplifted.

Keeping arms raised, eyes closed, tear streamed faces mumbling "Thank You Jesus" took stamina. As each praying sibling tired, I could see arms had lowered. Muscles trembled in short spasms then relaxed. Open palms would be shoulder high but gradually slipped lower. Mouths voicing prayers emitted softer sounds. Unintelligent mumbles. But then dad would soon descend from the pulpit stage where he had dozed and nodded seated in the thronelike chair. With a long, narrow switch, dad seemed in a mischievous mood, behaving like a mean teenager. If someone had stopped praying, or hands not open and outstretched, that switch was playfully administered. Worst would happen if a person was caught asleep. Dad would then administer the full force of the switch. He was like a jockey urging horses. Blows from being struck, and his loud voice, would be enough to make our praying voices rise louder like cresting waves and falling crescendos. He was the coach, circus man, god's lion tamer.

"PRAY! DON'T LET THE DEVIL USE YOU! PRAY! PUT ON THE WHOLE ARMOR OF GOD! NO SLEEPING!"

This time dad's thundering words were followed by two lashes of the switch on my shoulder. I felt the sharp stings and my voice was louder more from surprise than pain. My arms had been uplifted while voicing my praying words. My verbal focus was on evil doers in the world. Bullies.

Teachers who dispensed unfair grades. Employers who refused to hire. Still I had been struck by dad's enforcement rod. His justification quickly followed.

"No improvising! No asking for worldly things! Just say Thank You Jesus! Express gratitude that you are alive! Be happy that you can suffer for his sake!"

This ordeal was six days a week. I knew that it made no sense to protest. I was the eldest and dad was making an example out of me. Avoidance could only happen if I had an evening part- time job.

Other church attendees outside our family routinely arrived on the scene much later.

Weekly evening worship services officially started at 7:30 pm, but other folks usually arrived shortly after 8:00 p.m. Their timing was such as to miss the long tortuous prayer periods. They never saw the dad's switch action. However, like ourselves, they were greeted by smells of olive oil administered on foreheads, and furniture polish on the twelve rows of wooden chair racks. Maybe they ignored the dust from the threadbare carpet covering cold concrete. They came just in time for a brief five to six minutes of praying. Singing and sermonettes would shortly follow. I was glad when outsiders, non-family attendees arrived. This meant the praying would soon end, and the physical punishments stop. Dad's switch disappeared. However, for us family members forced to open the church doors and start the so-called Prayer Services, it was pure torture. Our father preached that serving god was for all to "freely" come. But over the years one thing was clear. There was nothing "free" about these forced worship activities. Suffering was something we all were being conditioned to accept.

When prayer service ended Dad started a hymn. If the pianist or organ player had not arrived, dad thumped the piano himself. Most Friday nights his song choice was the up-tempo lyrics: "I was glad when they said unto me, let us go into the house of the lord!" This song had a fast, handclapping 4/4th beat. The late comers would rise from their knees smiling and handclapping to the beat. Happiness was not the case for family members who had been praying a longer period. Fatigued trembling muscles and numb limbs were familiar sufferings. I felt relief mixed with resignation. The song I sang was a lie. I was not glad being forced into church attendance virtually seven days a week. I was not glad being forced to pray in uncomfortable positions under a threat of being struck with belt or switch.

These worship services never ended without the church pastor singing two or more blood themed songs. Among my fathers' favorites were: *"The Blood of Jesus"*, and *"Power In the Blood"*. All behaviors from our pastor father had been justified by snippets and phrases from the Holy Bible. Whippings, forced singing, and long and loud uncomfortable praying. We were constantly reminded to be willing sacrifices. I silently prayed to find a means for escaping this madness.

For a while it seemed wise to not fight, go with the flow. In San Bernardino I soon became a church youth leader. Months later my position rose to Deacon status. This move became protection from dad's corporal punishments, but he had shown other attempts at maintaining attention as well as control. Dad became a standup comedian on the church pulpit. When it ever became apparent that most of the congregation of 25 souls, including our family, were not paying attention, the real show began. Assuming the role of an agitated prospective convert resisting joining our faith, dad would use a high-pitched falsetto voice. His large wrists would become limp as he switched his body and shrugged his shoulders. His female parody…

We died from laughter, sometimes even falling out of our seats. These moments of levity were in great contrast to Dad's normal stiff seriousness.

Flip Wilson's popular *Geraldine* character had stiff competition.

✳✳✳✳✳

The closer we came to the Nebraska state line, a nagging worry surfaced. In the back of my mind was a fear that the Newton's, a white family, may have a great amount of curiosity about our sudden marriage. I had never mentioned VJ all two years I had lived in Nebraska. Also, their daughter Kristen, might have been upset because on my last visit I had galloped her injured horse for miles over the plains. The horse had been recovering from a leg injury. Kristen had been absent and the mother suggested that of their three horses this would be most gentle.

Just walk it slowly, Sissie had advised, it's not ready to go fast. But I had returned that horse to the stall fully lathered and panting.

We had not spoken since my last visit. The warm welcome on this return surprised me.

"Ah! You made it! Welcome! Welcome! And this is your new bride! She is so beautiful! Well done!"

Sissie Newton looked at VJ giving her a huge smile. Then her gaze swept us both as we moved toward her and exchanged warm hugs. Her two young daughters and husband stood stiffly nearby smiled sheepishly.

"Do let us take your luggage. Ted and the girls will handle that. Follow me, let me show you to your room. We are so glad you made it safely. It's a long drive from California. Come on now." I took VJ's hand and we walked into the large expansive ranch style house. We were in Elkhorn, Nebraska on the Newton Family homestead called "Coast Ridge". This was several miles from Omaha. We were about halfway through our Journey to downstate Bloomington, Illinois.

Our hosts were a white family. Sissie befriended me after my poetry performance at High School in a small Nebraskan town. Her daughter attended Wesleyan University, the same college as myself, in Lincoln. Apparently, she had told her mother about me and I had participated in her poetry show at the Joslyn Art Museum in Omaha. Ted, Sissie's Husband, has given her this gift as a birthday present to showcase her original work. We had many practice sessions, and for that program wore customized outfits: all white slacks and shirts, with sky blue satin sashes. The readings were accompanied with Chamber music: violins and flute. One particular poem I enjoyed reciting was *"Stairs to Nowhere"*. It pains me because to this day I had not located that piece.

While staying this time at Coast Ridge, Sissie was curious about my decision to leave Seminary in Indianapolis. Her brief questions I handle with brevity, not wanting to spoil our festive moods.

"So, tell my why the sudden move to leave Indianapolis and return to Grad school in Illinois. That's so different?" From the sound in her voice I figured this level of curiosity merited a serious response. I tried to keep it as light as possible.

"Well, Naptown was quite a change from Lincoln, Nebraska, but not that much. But I really needed a change. Tired of snow and cold weather." By the expression on her face I could tell Sissie was not going to let me skate by with superficiality.

"Come on Aaron... forget about the weather. Changing from Seminary to Mass Communications studies are quite different. You know what I mean." There was a long silence as I glanced at the fully attentive, expectant faces around the dinner table. Sissie pressed further hitting a hot button.

"What does your father think about this decision? You remember we all met at that small church after your graduation? What did your mother say? And I'm sure marrying a Catholic must not have set too well with them. Am I right?" I swallowed while shooting a quick help me glance at VJ. She smiled slightly and nodded while raising a quick eyebrow. I would try to sound as diplomatic as possible. Leaning forward I spoke with heightened earnestness.

"Actually, my parents have always said to do what makes me happy. And in all honesty, I just was not comfortable attending CTS in Indianapolis. I was expecting something more professional. Although the campus has state of the art communication facilities, there were too many things that made my fit there a mismatch." I sat back in my chair feeling that I had closed the question. There was a moment of silence and then VJ tossed in a topic change.

"We are so excited about be able to get a fresh start. There is so much that we can do being away from family and all..." The table was quiet for a nanosecond as Sissie's eyes darted from both VJ and I like watching a ping-pong match. However, the perplexed look on the face of our wise hostess told me that she was not satisfied but could go with the flow. But, since no one else picked up the ball her response was semi-hot-button question. Settling sharp gray eyes on VJ. With both eyebrows raised she then inquired:

"So… what are you going to do… down in Illinois? Are you going to also be working on your degree?"

My wife was quick and ready for this. "Oh-hhh, I plan on being busy. I am a certified teacher and can easily find work in Child Care. Then after he… my husband finishes, we've agreed that I will complete my next degree. We're ready. We'll be fine."

*****

What I did not tell Sissie about my Seminary discomfort became racial matters. Namely I had discovered that people supported the continued enslavement of Black folk using biblical justifications. Also, there was much hypocrisy concerning race-mixing in various fundamental denominations. And I was still trying to get my own head around the lack of interest of many Black churches to shoulder the push for social justice. I was silent. More than this, however, were personal events while in Indiana that led me to believe that my whole ontology and spiritual perspective was out of balance.

While at Wesleyan, breaking away from my past conditioning had been a slow learning process. First, there was relief to be able to fully immerse myself into studies without interruptions.

There were less mandatory church obligations. Second, there was less likelihood of being criticized about my reading or music listening choices. I recalled questioning dad about why he did not approve of my listening to the Mormon Tabernacle choir album I had purchased. "They are not true believers," he said, "I will not have devil music in my house." He also had already made it clear what he thought about rock n roll, and jazz. "If you insist on playing spiritual garbage, you'd better find somewhere else to live. There's only one man in this house!" He was hard-nosed about this. His opinion was not to be defied. It was not clear how he had decided that sonatas and rhapsodies by Mozart and Beethoven, whom he played on piano, were holier than Count Basie or Ramsey Lewis's jazz. These unresolved issues I had settled when entering Wesleyan University. However, I would soon be shamed out of my one-track-mental- conditioning by real-life experiences shortly after graduation.

My only real link to my past in the west was a chance meeting with a former student from San Bernardino high. Norris Gregory had been a Junior, in the class behind me. He was a yellow skinned, always jovial, smiling, black kid, the only child of prominent parents in the community. Norris was on the tennis, golf, swim, and B-basketball teams. He drove a sporty 1957 Thunderbird coupe. In his senior year he was elected the first black mayor of San Bernardino high. Successfully gaining entrance to Harvard I envied his achievements. However, while in junior college I had inherited his white debate partner from high school. During our brief surprise encounter in an airport I asked him about Harvard.

"Hey man! How's it going, do you like being in that ivy league school?" Immediately his face became crestfallen. He stopped smiling after our pleasantries. His response surprised me.

"I hate it. I wish that I had made a different choice." This response completely baffled me.

Everyone thought going to Harvard was the pinnacle to success. This is what our teachers had said. We did not have time to delve into what he really meant. After good lucks and handshakes Norris was gone. About five years later reading that Norris had allegedly committed suicide caused me to take a serious pause about my own inner versus other-directed goals. Norris, in my opinion, had had it all and was poised for greater successes. However, the stresses that went along with being a token, or in hostile environments take their toll. I could not afford being like a wind-up toy, mechanically charging into meaningless corners. Superstitious chants and rituals needed re-examination for pause, repair, or removal.

For several years after Wesleyan, Sissie Newton kept in contact exchanging letters. Her exquisite handwriting reflected artistry, patience, and care. No matter how long, several pages or short cards, her penmanship were works of art.

In one particular letter were words that made my thinking rise above narrow-minded navel-gazing....

We stayed only two days in Coast Ridge, despite being pressed to remain longer. I was determined to reach our final destination intact. I had reminded VJ that although we had been served breakfasts in bed, this was not to be construed as our Honeymoon. However, the Newton's have a special place in my heart. I am proud to say that I knew them. One important lesson I learned from this relationship was that a person could be spiritually minded without torture or attacking other people about theological beliefs. Actions are the most compelling sermons.

CHAPTER 14

A Diplomacy Kitchen

One particular neighbor girl in Indianapolis was cute. She had large friendly hazel eyes, small freckles sprinkled like brown sugar on cream colored skin. Her lips and cherub like cheeks forecasted a predictable smile. In this city I had met, Laurene, a white Canadian social worker, after graduating from Wesleyan University in Nebraska. I was our family's first college graduate, and I had no intention of returning home to evangelical prison life in California. I travelled to Indianapolis, where I enrolled in the Christian Theological Seminary (CTS). My hope was to kill two birds with one stone: (1) keep my parents soothed in believing I was following my father's footsteps to become a man of the cloth; (2) and remain one step ahead of the military draft. Higher education was a legitimate way to avoid joining the continued conflict in Vietnam.

The social climate between blacks and whites was very tense across the country. In the city of Indianapolis, episodes of police brutality were very real and frequent.

This included anti-war battles between long-haired "Hippies" Doves versus Hawks.

Working as a community park sports coach for the Social Service center I saw Lorene on rare occasions. Occasionally, we hit tennis balls or went to movies. Being that she was Canadian, at the time, I had not foreseen any problem with our socializing. However, her being Catholic would eventually be my hang-up.

In Indianapolis, I split my Sundays between a Methodist church and a Pentecostal church. I worked with the Methodist youth group and sang in the Pentecostal choir, occasionally preaching sermonettes. Minister Grace, one of three competing Pentecostal church leaders in the city, helped me find a place to stay. He was very conservative and old- school, so it was critical that I not appear to be a revolutionary or hippie.

At our first meeting, he got right down to business. "Young man, you're 'Saved' aren't you?" he asked as I was nervously seating myself.

"Yes, sir," I respectfully replied. This was a screening interview. His stern eyes probed as he quizzed me further.

"And you really love the Lord?"

"With all my heart." My saying these words I knew were expected tradition and rituals.

A few more simple questions and the preacher seemed satisfied.

"That's good, that's good. Seeing as how you're not married and still a virgin, I have a living arrangement in mind for you that would be a good thing. It's with an old widow. She complains that 'villains' are trying to enter her house at night. Her hearing isn't too good, so I'm not so sure about that. You can help her out a little. Just give her a few dollars each week for rent. Are you good with this?"

"Sounds alright with me." I could barely keep my voice from sounding overly excited.

Minister Grace also seemed relieved.

"Good! She could use the money, and the whole area will be safer with your presence. You might even be able to use your car to bring her to church with you on Sunday. That is, if you don't mind. God is love, you know."

I met Widow B. Belle after church the next Sunday. She was a small, almond-colored, beetle-eyed woman. Remaining stone-faced, she scrutinized me for several minutes through her plastic, horn-rimmed eyeglasses that kept fogging up before uttering a word. Her eyes peered through rimless glasses perched on her small nubby nose. A dark-brown, oily curled salt-and-pepper wig perched on her small, birdlike head.

She had lived alone ever since her husband had died fifteen or twenty years earlier.

They had been together in Indiana's capitol city, happy and childless for thirty-five years before that. He had worked for the Indiana Railroad as a steward. Widow Belle had not worked since her marriage. Within the first three minutes of meeting anyone, she would inform them that 'her Herbert' had been a good man. In a wise, soft, reedy voice, she would repeat, "He was a clean penny! Praise god! A clean penny!"

Of course, no one disputed this statement. She had no neighbors, as the lots on either side of her home were vacant and zoned for commercial use. Widow Belle cherished her privacy and had no thought of change. However, Minister Grace somehow convinced her to give up her privacy to 'help the poor boy out.' It seems like we were both being foisted off on each other out of charity.

The inside of Widow Belle's house was stuffy. A strong musty smell of old damp clothes pervaded it, like an attic with no ventilation. The strong fragrance of mothballs, ammonia, bleach, and cleaning solvents suggested that cleaning and mopping were among her favorite activities.

Looking around, I saw that an unwelcome intrusion from "villains" was highly unlikely. Widow Belle's home was like a bunker of triple locks and double-window-paned readiness. A boldly lettered *BEWARE OF DOG* sign out front encouraged others to think twice before entering. In addition, her constant loud praying and appearance were off-putting. She endlessly shuffled from room to room. The wig was usually askance because there were no mirrors in her home. She would drag a long wooden baseball bat behind her. She spent her time idly rearranging her glass menagerie of figurines in various nooks and crannies, peering out the windows, and re-examining her door locks. Her deceased husband's double-barreled shotgun leaned behind her bedroom door. She kept it dusted and oiled, yet insisted, "I'm not shooting up no gun. That's against the Bible. This bat is well enough the 'rod of correction,' and it'll surely do God's work if push comes to shove! Praise god! I'm not a fool."

Her reedy voice always sounded calm and mellow, like a wise gnome in a cartoon.

Although, the Jackson Five and George Benson were homegrown local favorites, only gospel music played on her radio. She wore the same plain, loose, old house dress every day because she seldom left the house. The only exception was on special Sundays or when local churches had special interchurch music programs. On these occasions, she'd don a wide-brimmed hat and hitch a ride from one of her friends who only ever called her on the phone.

She preferred staying at home and listening to Billy Graham's radio sermons, which she argued with and complained about: "That boy still trying to preach? He just doesn't read his Bible right. I don't know what folks see in that white man. Praise God! They ought to let Bishop on that station. Praise God! Of course, that would take a whole lot of money. Black folk don't have no money."

She was referring to Bishop "Sin-Killing" Sanders, a prominent leader of the Pentecostal Assemblies. He was a short, mean, West Indian man. He was deeply conservative and embraced Old Testament severity and punishments. A legend among the old schoolers. He seldom smiled, and his close-cropped gray hair, heavily lined face, and trim gray moustache made him look a bit like the Grim Reaper. Most people steered clear of this grave man, giving him a wide berth more out of fear than admiration. However, Widow Belle admired him.

In my naiveté, I once made the mistake of approaching him and asking him, "Why do the black and white Pentecostal churches have separate organizations?"

His response was cold and dismissive: "These matters do not concern you. Let your leaders deal with such things and focus on saving yourself. That's what you should do: save Yourself!" His stern, glaring eyes were not friendly, and the bitter look on his face terminated the hope of any further conversation. The few lay folk listening nearby quickly scuttled away like beetles suddenly under intense light.

Despite Widow Belle's respect for Bishop Sanders, when I told her about this exchange, she exclaimed, "That's rubbish! God said we are all one, and we should worship him as one.

Praise god! I study my Bible, too, and I can read it just as well as he can. He ain't no pretty penny, that's for sure! Praise god! Not a pretty penny."

Despite having a key to the outer door, I still needed to ring the doorbell to get in the second door. Widow Belle would then slowly remove the sliding bolt and chain, just barely open the door, scrutinize me with roving eyes, and sniff me with her nubby nose before letting me in. Surprisingly, there was a lightness in her attitude of surveillance, scrutiny, and criticism. Her entire bearing had a certain comical levity when she assured me, "I'm just keeping an eye on you, young man. The Devil is busy, and we must always be vigilant. Praise God! Did you lock that other door behind you?"

Widow Belle was simple and old-school. She often complained about "some foolishness on the radio," "the television idiot box," and noise from traffic outside, commenting, "We didn't have all this ruckus when horses and buggies were around. No sir! But I will not let these changes ever interrupt me from studying my Bible. Praise god!"

To be fair, she did have a point about the traffic on Indiana Avenue, where the house was located. The street was just off Meridian Boulevard, the main avenue running through the city, where speeding was just a natural part of life.

I believed Widow Belle to be kind and with good intentions. Aside from her constant vigilance and unending telephone conversations with her friends, she lived what many people her age would call a "holy life." She spent most of her day reading the Bible and in prayer.

When her late husband's retirement pension check arrived each month, she paid one-tenth to Minister Grace's church as a tithe. Whenever Girl Scouts were bold enough to ignore the NO PEDDLERS OR SOLICITORS sign on her door, she bought cookies from them. Her act of taking me in and disrupting her solitude was a big move of generosity, especially since I paid just twenty dollars a week for my room.

I attempted to return her kindnesses and appreciated her allowing me a small space in her refrigerator to store my milk, juice, and leftovers in Tupperware containers. I did not respond to her complaints about my using too much hot water when showering. I even attempted to accommodate her dislike for the "questionable" music I played.

One night, I was listening to the vocal group The Fifth Dimension's song "One Less Bell to Answer" in my room. I had the sound so low, it was barely audible, even with my ear pressed close to the speakers. Being hard of hearing, I was sure, she couldn't hear it. And yet, she suddenly knocked on my door. "That's not modern church music, is it?"

"No, Sister Belle. This is a new group I like," I explained.

"Well, whatever it is, I can still hear. It's not gospel song. Please turn it down." Her irritation spoke volumes. I knew she meant it was devil music. The volume was so low, the needle scratching the record surface could be hear above the words. But I remained polite. She was old school, and this was her house. "Yes, m'am. Just five more minutes, and I'll turn it off for the night."

"I really don't like that kind of music in my house, but good night!" Those sharp-edged words stung.

Another time, I tried being helpful driving her shopping for her groceries. Unfortunately, she was not methodical—or quick— in this activity. Widow Belle took her time peering at the molasses and syrup bottles bearing the smiling face of Aunt Jemima before selecting the type she always used. Upon reaching the shelves filled with hot and cold cereals, she spent a good five-to-ten minutes examining boxes before slowly placing her usual Corn Flakes and Cheerios in her cart alongside the bold red, white, and blue tubular oatmeal container featuring a smiling Puritan man with the long white hair.

Widow Belle insisted on placing all these items in the cart herself. She did not allow me to touch her choices. It was clear that my generous effort of helping with the grocery-shopping expedition was not going smoothly. "Stop rushing me," she kept repeating. "I've got a long list. Is there somewhere else you've got to be? You can go on ahead. I'll find another ride home." If she had a list, it was entirely inside her head.

Despite her kindness, Widow Belle was also a trying roommate. On occasion, she would open my bedroom door without knocking. Sticking her head in my room, she would peer around and say, "Ah, there you are! Praise god! I was just making sure you were alone. Good night." Then she'd leave, closing the door behind her.

And then there were her friends. She spent hours on the phone with various fellow widows sharing gossip, discussing community events, and making decisions about the menu for their weekly potluck gatherings. One day, I made the mistake of coming home around dinner time. Unbeknownst to me, this was during Widow Belle's turn to host such an event. Nine or ten black women were nosily chatting away in the dining room. Widow Belle unlocked the second door to usher me inside.

There was a sudden silence, and all gaiety and laughter immediately halted as she brought me center stage and made introductions. The choking aroma of feminine perfumes gagged me, and a creeping feeling of nausea was in my throat. Piercing eyes scrutinized me from head to toe. The traffic noises outside vanished. Even the loud cawing black crows lined up in rows on the telephone wires outside could not be heard. All was drowned out by a group of old, black, harpies discussing me amongst themselves. These women talked as if I was invisible, yet shot a few question my way.

"Oh, he's such a young thing!" "Such a handsome young man!"

"I sure could put some more meat on his bones, I tell you!"

"Young man, where are your parents from again? New York? I've got some people up there. Do you know the Armstrong family?"

"No, girl, he said California. Now, I got folk out there. Son, do you know the Williamses?

Now they got a large family. The father works for the Kaiser hospital. Do you know them?"

"You got a lot in your family—fifteen kids? Your mother must really be a workhorse. I can't imagine having so many."

"Why don't you sit down here and have a bite to eat with us? We ain't gonna hurt you." "Naw, honey, we don't bite! He-he-he!"

"You got a girlfriend? I got a nephew whose daughter is 'bout your age. You should meet her."

"No, this one here is 'saved.' He's studying to be a preacher! He ain't got time to be running 'round, chasing skirts. He be fasting and prayin', Lord have mercy!"

"Come on, honey! Eat up now, you hear? You need more meat on them bones of yours.

You gotta be strong!"

"Yes, Lord! It's not just us old folk who are the 'salt of the earth,' you know what I'm saying?"

I hurriedly scarfed the plate of food that was offered, then stood to take my empty plate into the kitchen. The gentle voice of Widow Belle interrupted my actions. "Oh no, no, no! You don't need to be doing that," she declared. "I'll take care of the dirty dishes. You're still my guest! You sit down and relax. Chat with us old women for a spell… unless you have a date or something. Praise god!" Taking this opportunity to speak, I sought a quick exit.

"Actually, I have homework I need to do, so if you all will pardon me, I must be going.

It's been a pleasure meeting you all," I said as politely as I could.

"Same here, honey, same here. The pleasure has been all ours. It ain't every day that we women get to sit down and have a meal wid' a fine gentleman like yourself. Am I right, girls? I know I'm right."

"Yes, old Belle's been hogging you all to herself. Child, I'm gonna be frank: I am so jealous!"

"Can't you give us a little hug before you go?"

"Yes, you don't need to be listening to old lady talk. You should be out there!"

The women burped and laughed with delight as I made my exit. Widow Belle wore a mischievous smirk on her face. Her gerbil-like countenance gleamed, and her crab-like eyes rolled in a slow happy dance.

A few days later, I brought Laurene to the house after we had played tennis on the courts across the street. Arthur Ashe had just won the U.S. Tennis Open, and he had inspired me to become the next black tennis star, despite my lack of training. I purchased equipment but had no clue and no coach. Laurene, a co-worker from Canada, offered to show me some basics, so we started playing together. Our tennis games were terrible, but I felt comfortable with her, and we could talk about non-religious topics. Those issues, by now, were tedious and bored me. I did not like being a one-track minded evangelist.

There were no drinking fountains at the small park, and one day, we forgot to bring water bottles. Since I lived right across the street, it seemed practical to just go get some water there.

Inside the house, the overpowering smell of ammonia and mothballs still caused me to hold my breath for a few seconds upon first entering, but Laurene did not appear to notice.

Much to my surprise, Widow Belle was not at home, so we poured ourselves some water from the tap. I led her to my room so I could proudly show off my new SONY record player.

Listening to a few cuts from *The Fifth Dimension* record album with the volume up was a real treat for me. I played the song "Puppet Man" twice, and we laughed and crooned along with Marilyn MacKoo singing "One Less Bell to Answer." I told Laurene, "I can't really play this when the old lady is here." "Really? You're kidding me!" Laurene was surprised. "Nope."

Finally, we headed back down to the kitchen to dispose of our drinking cups. While so doing, sounds from the front of the house indicated that someone was entering. For a moment, I panicked: had I forgotten to lock the doors behind me? I was sure that I had secured at least one of them. I heard slow dragging footsteps and then silence. I shot a glance at Laurene and then proceeded on to the kitchen.

"What are you doing in my kitchen?" Widow Belle snapped when she saw us, her heavy wooden bat cradled in the crook of one arm. She peered at us through her frosty eyeglasses, her eyes rolling wildly like a disoriented crab. Her voice was accusatory.

"Oh, it's you, Sister Belle," I said, exhaling in relief. "You had me worried for a minute there. I thought some intruder had gotten inside. I knew I had locked at least one door."

"I see. Well, the only intruder I see is with you. I want to know what this woman is doing in my kitchen."

"We were playing tennis across the street and got thirsty. Is it a crime to offer my guest a drink of water?" I asked.

"Listen, young man. You know I don't want nobody coming into my house when I'm not here. This is not a public community meeting room. I can't have that," she said, her voice firm.

"Sister Belle, let me introduce my friend," I said, trying to smooth things over. "This is Laurene Peters, my co-worker at the social service center. Laurene, meet my landlady, Sister B. Belle. We go to the same church."

Widow Belle then provided the usual essential information: "You should know that my husband passed away fifteen-twenty years ago. I never needed to work after marrying him. He gave me everything I needed. Everything."

Several seconds of uncomfortable silence passed as the two women stoically exchanged plastic smiles, deflecting more than the generational gap. The tension had not eased. Between the young white and senior black females there was no more pretense at social niceties, only a stony stare-down. We quickly headed for the front door while Widow Belle replaced her bat in her bedroom. She then stood in the hallway, hands on hips. As I followed Laurene out, Widow Bellow's voice caught my ear: "Young man, we're gonna have to have a talk when you get back. Praise god!"

At Laurene's car, the two of us burst out laughing. "What was that? Did you see her face?" she giggled. "You would have thought she was going to have a conniption."

"Yes, she's pure OG, that's for sure. I kinda like the old lady, though. She's strange, yet wise. I just don't like the way she seems to hover around me all the time, trying to mother me. I'm too old for a mother. I can't even listen to my own music because it's always 'too loud.'"

"And what's with that bat?" Laurene asked.

"She claims that in the past, some druggies or drunks tried to break in. I guess it's no secret that she's an old lady living alone."

"True. Still, it might be time for you to look for your own place." She paused then added, "Not to be rude, but... that smell! I can't see how you put up with it. Can I tell you something? At the office, they call you 'Mothballs.' Now I see why."

"You're kidding!"

"Nope."

"Well, to tell you the truth, whenever she unlocks the door to let me in, she sniffs around, as if trying to detect something. Once, she even asked me if I had been smoking. Another time, she asked if I had been drinking. I don't do either one. It's really a pain to be scrutinized like that all the time."

"Yeah, like I said, it might be time to move on. Maybe you've worn out your welcome."

Later that evening, after having dinner in a nearby Chinese restaurant with Laurene, I returned to the house. Widow Belle was silent when I walked in. She allowed me ten minutes to get settled in before coming to my room and beginning her attack: "What is wrong with you?

Don't you have any sense at all? Praise god! Don't you know better than to be bringing a white woman into my kitchen? I am thoroughly disappointed in you. Apparently, your mother did not teach you anything."

"Well, I know you'll be praying for us both," I said evenly.

"Don't talk to me about praying. You better pray for yourself. And maybe it's time for you to start looking for somewhere else to live. Pray that you can find one as good as you already have. Hear me?"

I was actually relieved at her words. "I suppose you're right. I should leave while we're still on good terms."

"Young man, I like you. I really do. But it would be best for you to find your own place. Just let me know when you're leaving. And I'll want my key back. You know God is love!"

This was a familiar platitude, but I had no idea what she had meant. By now I had become tired and frustrated. Tired of living a double life like a spy in two warring camps. Believers versus non-believers. It was increasingly frustrating to claim to believe in things that seemed superstitious at best. That kitchen situation marked one more nail in the coffin of Holy Rollers. I hope to find a graceful way the exit the fringe.

CHAPTER 15

SHAME AND CHANGE

Hustling for money without fear of public ridicule was one lesson I learned from the truck escapades with my father. However, facing fear and anxiety was what I had failed to do when push came to shove. My failure to compete in the important High school tournament could not be blamed on my parents. I had to face the fact of being ashamed to take the way out that had presented itself to potentially solve my dilemma. My no showing up reflected the depth and lack of my commitment. In hindsight, taking an honest look at myself in a subsequent event revealed my blindness. What happened to me one afternoon while standing on Capitol Street in Indianapolis would be a crucial turning point in my life.

After graduation and moving to Indianapolis, one life experience gave me a vicious stomach punch. I had just cashed a check for six-hundred dollars. This money was an emergency loan from the Seminary to purchase an automobile. After stashing the bulk of the money in my briefcase, I grabbed a quick hamburger from McDonald's. My stomach had reminded me it was well past lunch time. Then I headed for the bus benches with briefcase in hand. While waiting for the bus, hopefully for the last time, two individuals approached me. A young Black couple. The man was tall, slim and of medium brown complexion. His slightly smaller female companion was lighter skinned and shapely. The man spoke first.

"Pardon me young man, can you tell us where a shoe store is? *Footwear*, you heard of that place? We're in a hurry and need to buy our son some shoes."

His voice was low, pleasant, articulate and polite. Appearance clean and non-threatening. I paused momentarily from looking down the street to see if the bus was approaching. It was not in sight. Directing full attention to this couple I replied.

"Sorry, I don't know where *Footwear* is, but you might try that direction. Lots of stores over there." I pointed toward the business center. The couple thanked me, smiled and took a few steps in the direction I had pointed. In that instant a young Black male, a few inches shorter than myself, approached me. His clothing disheveled, hair uncombed, in an obvious spirit of desperation. He came close almost bumping into me. "Please! Please! Can you help me please? I am lost! My brother died in a job accident. I have just collected his insurance money. I need to find this address." He had tears in his eyes. Panic in his voice. African accent. Obviously, a foreigner. Thrusting a crumpled strip of paper with a note scribbled on it, he pointed at faint street name and numbers. I stared at him dumbfounded for a second. Then peered at his note squinting my eyes. It was hard to read in the brilliant afternoon sunlight. I shook my head indicating regret. In that moment of hesitation, he flashed a look of disappointment, and turned to the young couple who were now about two steps away. Pulling out a hand from his pocket that clutched a thick wad of dollar bills, he addressed the man and lady. He thrusted the money and scribbled note at them, while looking back at me. His eyes kept me hooked while he spoke to them.

"Please help me find this address! I am new to this country and need directions!" The couple also seemed momentarily startled. Looking at me they ushered him back toward me. Closer. In a small public huddle the woman now spoke. "Is this your friend? What does he want?" The tall slim man then added a warning of caution, fastening his gaze on both me and the African foreigner. His voice was now intense, a secretive hushed tone. "Man... you'd better put that money away! Don't you know it's dangerous to be flashing money like that out here? What's wrong with you?" Addressing me directly he continued. "You should talk to your friend. Help him." Immediately I tried to put the brakes on the assumptions and misunderstanding. "Sorry, I do not know him… he's not…" But I was interrupted by the woman.

"Look, we don't have time for this. We don't know him either. Why don't you help him?" The slim man added, "My wife and I are on our way to buy our son some shoes. We're on the clock, paying a baby-sitter. You live around here don't you?" I was becoming agitated. I glanced at the bus stop. It had not arrived. "No…" "Are you going to work, or a student?" "Yes, I'm a student. I told you already I am not familiar with this area." The interview was quick, like a fast pepper interrogation. A mix of foot traffic, mostly White folk, hurriedly passed by our group. I took a step backwards and the three individuals came closer as if I was a magnet. The next question came from the lady. "Where do you go to school?" I looked at her and proudly responded. "CTS. *Christian Theological Seminary.*" The group seemed relieved as the couple smiled and the African foreigner exhaled with a sigh of relief. "Oh, good! You're a Christian. He can trust you. Why don't you want to help him? You're a Christian aren't you? Have you read about the good Samaritan?" Asked the slim man. Then lady interrupted before I could answer, "We can help only if you help. We can't just leave your brother alone like this. If you sacrifice your time so will we. Let's go sit down somewhere in public and figure this thing out. What do you say?"

I glanced again toward the bus stop. The bus had already arrived, double doors were closing. I thought about running to catch it, bang on the windows. But then it struck me that this would not be Samaritan like behavior. A Christian running away from a man in need. Cowardly.

Pushing back my feelings against bolting was a struggle. I thought about Pedro Blanco, the foreigner who years ago I had only partially helped. I could have prevented the thumb tack attack.

Now, a foreigner in front of me still had his money out while we talked. He fingered the thick wad that looked like hundred-dollar bills. He was a potential victim. I gestured sternly for him to put it back in his pocket. Our group huddled together as a rush of pedestrians flowed around us with mild curiosity and ambivalence.

A short time later, the four of sat cozily in a nearby coffee shop. After some brief pleasantries to break the ice it was determined that Slim would go with the foreigner to find the address. I was designated to hold his money until they returned. The woman would wait with me. "You have an honest face, and you are Christian so we trust you", they said. After several minutes had passed, the woman excused herself to answer nature's call in the coffee shop public restroom. She never returned. I waited and waited. The man and the foreigner also did not return. I opened the packet I held discovering in shock it held nothing more than cut-up newspaper strips. My money was also gone. I was traumatized and then furious. Hours later the police informed me that I had been victim of what is known as a "Pigeon Drop". One officer said, "This trio have been hitting the entire Indianapolis area like a storm. We have received several complaints about the people you described. Can't catch 'em. Their timing is impeccable. One thing for sure, you probably saw one of the best performances of your life. But you really paid for it. Six hundred dollars is a lot of money to lose!"

I kicked myself for being so naïve and trusting. I hated the fact that my need to appear and show "Christian" behaviors had cost me: pride and economic loss. I would be walking for several more months. Clearly Christian living meant suffering. Increasingly I hated this thought. I hated the label but was not clear about what hat or mask to wear that represented my identity.

CHAPTER 16

CONVERSION CLOSER

"Come on! Don't quit now!

Say Thank you, Jesus! Thank you, Jesus! Give up to God! Say it faster! Mean it!"

I was kneeling alongside an older married man. I was the last leg of what had started as the tag- relay praying team. Our now knees worn to the bone sore. From the dusty threadbare church carpet small puff of dust rose when our legs, knees, or feet shifted. It was crunch time. I could see he was near exhaustion and my job was to pull him through. I watched urging him on. His eyes were tightly closed, head sagging, body virtually limp. His once crisp clean white shirt was sweat soaked wringing wet. His efforts to keep his tongue moving had become weak, his fainter. He was fading fast. I could now barely hear his words, but his will to continue still weakly came through. My chants and prodding alternated in response to his faltering phrases.

"Th-th-thank you-u-u Jee-s-sus... Th-th-th- tank yo-you-Jee-s-sus..." I had to be more forceful.

"Come on! Louder! Praise God! Tell him you love him! Thank him! Louder! THANK JESUS! Come on!

"Thank you Jesus! Thank you Je-e-e-sus!" That's right. Faster now! Faster! COME ON BROTHER! "TH- THANK yo-o-u Jeee-s-u-us! TH-TH-TH-AAAANK youuuu....!"

"Come on! Brother! Come on! Thank him! You're almost there. Give up!! Give up to Jesus! Go! Go! Go!" I hammered hard those words and phrases. Over the years I had probably repeated the Thank you Jesus phrase at least a million times. I had the stamina to go all night if necessary. This process was a grueling "Tarry Service". Waiting for the spirit to engulf and control the new soul we soon hoped to join our religious faction. I had been trained well. This man was bound to become one of us. Other enablers, male and female saints, had already gone home. It was later after the sermon. This man had responded to the preacher's call to be saved. He had been baptized by submersion. The final step in his conversion was to induce him to speak in tongues. My job was to drive him to the brink of his will and self-control. If successful, he would become pliable like a newborn child. This we called his rebirth into a newer, brighter world.

This phase of conversion was vital to becoming a Holy Roller. A Saint. He must pray and wait to speak in tongues. At best this process usually involved few hours. At worst this tarrying could take days or months. It was a test of weakening a person's will power, physically and mentally. The effect was similar to putting a person in a small black box and draining his senses and emotions to go beyond the wall of self-control. A small group of believers volunteered to "pull new converts through". A church member's presence was required to verify the actual transition. I was the final member of the prayer tag-team. This was physically demanding work. But with my sports fitness background, I had stamina and could outlast newbies. I had done this ritual procedural work in other Pentecostal churches. Wearing a person down so control of senses, mind, body, especially verbal speech was vital. The human body eventually would respond like a computer that runs on autopilot. Soon the tongue would loosen up and verbal blabber would stream out. Uncontrollably. Words of many languages that even the speaker could not understand would spew forth. The target would thus enter the world of Holy Rollers. Religious scholars called this verbal spiritual break through *glossalalia*, i.e., speaking in tongues, i.e., several unknown languages. Such behavior

Pentecostals believed was the ultimate sign that the seeker had been anointed. He or she would then be considered "Saved". I continued my work yelling at the man. Urging him on. Louder.

"COME ON! SAY THANK YOU JESUS! JESUS! JESUS! THANK YOU! COME ON! GIVE UP TO GOD!"

I exhorted the man to give up his will and let the spirit have his body. Verbally pushing him beyond his current state of exhaustion. I must pull him past the physical and mental walls that urged him to stop. If my efforts were successful, my status among the church goers would rise. This achievement was like earning a patch in target-shooting or building a campfire out of two sticks. The work was just more rigorous like mountain climbing. However, for some reason that night, I noticed something about this man's behavior that differed from all my years of Tarrying experience.

*****

The married man gripped the thick gold wedding band on his left hand and slowly began twisting it off. Thank You Jesus phrases, alternated between loud, wailing and pleading, to faint whimpering gasps. This chanting would continue at least one hour or more. It all depended on his willingness to continue. Some people lasted three or four hours to become totally drained and willingly pliable to suggestions and commands. He was giving us permission to guide him into a new way. Unknown to him this would mean relinquishing his reasoning and decision- making to the stern dictatorial preacher, old man Greer.

His wife had been visited our church on several occasions. She was more attractive than the normal odd-ball types that usually filled Pentecostal congregations. I had heard a rumor that she had insisted that either her husband join this church, or their marriage would end. She was threatening divorce. She was clearly his pride and joy, and his actions were those of a desperate hostage being black mailed.

He was like a limp rag, he and elbow on the chair seat. His body virtually spayed on the floor. I placed my head closer to his ear like a detective extracting a confession. I cheered and exhorted him on with intense fervor. "Come on brother! You're almost there! Give up to Jesus! Give it all up!"

The man now had reached the final whimpering stage of tarrying process. He sobbed and pleaded between each word. I kept relentlessly pushing. Louder. Fierce with intensity. And then watched with amazement as he slowly pulled the gold wedding band off his finger

"Take my wife Jesus! Take my wife!"

Suddenly, the man collapsing into a heap on the floor entered a new dimension. His head rolled back and he began to speak in tongues. Wildly he suddenly moved his body reenergized. He thrashed and flung himself about as if possessed by a spirit. Clearly his movements were not under his own control. He rolled around on the floor as if wrestling unseen forces or beings.

While doing so he smiled and uttered gibberish opening his eyes that flashed wildly. This behavior continued until he was totally physically spent. My work was done. He would now be fully welcomed into the band of believers who cloaked themselves with a pious righteousness. My work was done.

On one hand I felt proud because I had been the one to pull him through. I had helped him reach the final step recruitment. The saints would look up to me with more esteem. However, on another level I felt less than proud and more guilt. This man would become our puppet. He would believe and do anything he was instructed if he was to remain "Saved". His mind would no longer be his own. This is what conversion was all about.

Meanwhile, I was becoming more conflicted by information from my bible research while at seminary. [Slavery + Violence + mysteries about early life of Jesus + hints of homosexuality = contradictory decrees by church leaders and splinter groups] I decided then to extract myself from this maddening life as a reluctant, flagging, evangelical robot. I would leave Indiana and start my life on a clean slate elsewhere. Soon I would find life in Illinois was radically different than Indiana although both were neighboring states. This state was also unlike living in California. None of this was like the cultures shock when transitioning from California to Nebraska.

CHAPTER 17

Black Clouds

[**1968] My nightmares had continued even after I moved away from home**, though they decreased in frequency.

As a student at Nebraska Wesleyan, I had been an assistant head dormitory resident, a researcher, and the president of Pho Rho Psi honorary speech fraternity. As a scholarship recipient, my responsibilities included participating in the intercollegiate debate team and individual speech competitions. Beyond that, Dr. Phil Kaye, the chair of the Speech Department granted me the freedom to plan my own course of study. He personally guided me to state championships and national finals and showed me the value of joining professional organizations.

He wasn't the only professor I had there who had a positive impact on me. Dr. Alice Jaswal, the debate team coach, welcomed my ideas and suggestions for our travelling debate team. Dr. DeGrazia, a professor of religious studies, challenged my notions of what it meant to be 'religious.' His comments about preferring to read my writings, rather than hearing my speeches gave me confidence to continue pursuing the craft I enjoyed most: writing. Dr. Julius Pfifer, a professor of philosophy, inspired in me a deep interest in the subject.

My independent research led me to read any and all black-related literature I could find: *Narrative of the Life of Frederick Douglass, an American Slave, Malcolm X, Soul On Ice* by Eldridge Cleaver, and anything about the Black Panther Party. My research soon came to focus on international student unrest. I could have never brought these books home in California without being attacked or vilified. However, being a student at Wesleyan, I also became involved with a theatrical production: a play called *The Visit*. I played a comedic duet role with another blind man. The almost entire white audience loved it, and together, we brought the house down. Participating in theater was also forbidden among the Pentecostals.

Aside from the fact of my continued college attendance in an institution run by "unbelievers," I committed three other small acts of defiance against the values of my upbringing.

My first defiant act was my attempt at dating. I viewed myself to be a naïve robot. I ached for worldly experiences. My romantic experience back home had been limited to sneaking some necking-time with Mattie, a girl at my church girl, so I didn't really know how to go about this whole social dating thing. I had never taken a girl out for a soda or a movie. Plus, during my first year in Nebraska, I was the only black male on campus. During my senior year, the freshman class had a handful of black student from Omaha, but I was several years older than them. I also started attending the small, cult-like storefront Pentecostal church in Lincoln. I made no secret of this, and invited some of my fellow students to attend. It was difficult for these Midwestern white students to even begin to understand what they had observed, and word soon got around campus about the wild emotional worship practices they had seen. This didn't help my dating, either.

I did pursue one girl, Terry, who was good company and a great conversationalist. We had met in the university piano practice rooms and were both musically-inclined. I enjoyed our time together and the limited escape from loneliness it offered, but these interactions were cut short when the campus chaplain approached me one day. "I would advise you to leave Terry alone. She is already engaged to someone else."

I was dumbfounded. Why had Terry never told me this? Trying to corner her and ask for an explanation seemed impossible. I never saw her practicing the piano again.

On a few occasions, dates involved off-campus dinners, trips to the off-campus ice cream parlor, or walks around the nearby residential neighborhood. These girls always insisted on bringing along another friend. After a few dates, they would give excuses of having too much homeworking and needing to study, and that was the end of that. In each instance, the size of my family eventually became an alarming issue, with comments of, "Oh my god! Your parents had fifteen children? I cannot imagine that! My goodness!"

It boiled down to my being an anomaly. I was a black guy in the Midwest, a member of a strange church, the product of a huge family. I was like a curious circus event. Being laughed at or treated with detached sympathetic mirth became tiring.

My second act of defiance happened after our thespian group celebrated the close of our last theatrical production. After strike, I brought a bottle of champagne to the group dinner. I had never consumed alcohol before, much less purchased any. Even at our church communion services, we only sipped grape juice. However, being twenty-four years old, I felt that having champagne at our dinner was the right thing to do.

Alcohol consumption was against campus rules, and even though our dinner took place off-campus, only a few of the students were over the legal drinking age of twenty-one. Most were Methodist kids from religious families. Thus, having the forbidden drink proved to be hilarious. The group wildly cheered when I produced the liquid surprise. I opened the champagne bottle with ease, and the liquid sprayed everywhere. The scene of young people hungrily trying to lap up puddles of booze was worth far more than the price of the champagne. It became obvious to me that I was not the only person who had been repressed.

My third recognizable act of defiance from my upbringing occurred around graduation. Rewarding myself for having successfully survived the university experience away from home, I purchased a small record player and a recording of jazz pianist Ramsey Lewis's music. I had heard him on radio and found inspiration in his creative versions songs I did not know as well as gospel songs rendered with extraordinary ingenuity. Worldly music became my salvation.

*****

[1969] I was an outsider in the Midwest. In Lincoln, Nebraska, I had to adjust to the sight of endless cornfields and the reality of snowy winters and learn how to walk on ice-covered sidewalks. I joined the dorm ritual of watching the *Johnny Carson Show* with younger boys in the recreation room. They knew when to say "Here's Johnny!" when their hometown hero came on.

During my second year there, the university increased its efforts to increase diversity on campus. Most of the new black freshmen they recruited were from Omaha's inner-city ghetto areas, and they struggled to find comfort on this small, virtually all-white campus.

The climate around the country was one of social unrest. Anti-war protests and Black Power chants filled the news. The popular music of the time reflected people on edge. From Nebraska's conservative capitol city, we watched events unfold in the larger and more diverse nearby city of Omaha. A barber in Omaha, Ernie Chambers, took the bull by the horns and became extremely vocal about police brutality and the lack of human rights for blacks in his city. On our campus administrators worried about potential ripple effects, especially since most of the new black students on campus were from Chambers' north Omaha area.

One day, an administrator approached me and asked, "Why do all the black students always eat together? Don't they know how to make friends with other students?" The role of social interpreter had been thrust upon me.

"The black students like to share and compare notes about their experiences. The whole phenomenon of being in a mostly white academic environment is new for them," I explained.

"But what do they talk about?" he continued. "Some people here are worried they may be plotting some kind of dangerous activity."

"Sorry, I don't know what they talk about. What do white students talk about when they eat together? Do you automatically think they're plotting some kind of revolution just because they eat in a group?" I countered.

"Do they have to look unfriendly, though? They never smile. People are afraid to approach them."

"They're young people away from home for the first time. Just being here has turned their world upside down. Plus, this structured learning environment demands that they be responsible for their own schedules and routines. They're stressed and nervous," I said.

Apparently, there were two sides to pursuing diversity on campus, and this became more apparent as low-level conflict broke out. A black student beat up a blind white student for bumping into him in the hallway. Another black student had to be hospitalized after running around campus naked one snowy winter night. Doctors determined that he had taken a heavy dose of LSD. I increasingly had to make it clear that I did not speak for the entire black community and that my opinions were only my own. After all, before coming to Nebraska, I had been raised in a virtual bubble, and my perspective was thus a narrow one. I knew nothing about race relations in Midwestern cities.

Travelling around the country with our debate team offered excitement and a chance to see more of the country and expand my views. I was the only person of color on our team, and sometimes that caused problems. One time, in Fort Worth, Texas, I stood in our hotel lobby, waiting for the rest of my team and our coach. Wearing a suit and tie, I also toted a briefcase with debate notes. Apparently, this was enough for several hotel guests to approach me, assuming I was on the staff:

"Can you bring my car around?" "Which way to the restaurant?"

"Can you take this luggage to our room?"

It was annoying. I finally learned to wait in an obscure location and pretend to read a newspaper.

On the other hand, my skin color resulted in a funny event during an excursion to Laredo, Mexico. Our car stopped at a school crossing where young kids, around seven or eight years old, stared at our vehicle with curiosity. They saw four pale white people, an unusual sight in this hot Mexican territory. A few braver boys moved closer, their hands cupped to their faces to shield their eyes while peering inside our car. Seeing me, a dark-skinned person, immediately struck them as funny. The kids must have thought I was an overcooked white person. They pointed and laugh heartily. More kids gathered around the car, and the laughter increased. To them, I was the funniest thing they had seen all day. I laughed in return and waved as we drove away. I saw the humor for what it was: I was an over-tanned novelty in these parts.

Back on campus, Karen, the alumni secretary, shared and unnerving story with me. A former black student at Nebraska Wesleyan, Joe Cowans, had graduated and gone back to his home state of New Jersey to earn a master's degree in math and science from Rutgers University. After that, he returned to Nebraska for medical school, where he worked with a white student colleague researching enzymes that affected mental retardation. Apparently, this was a break-though, cutting-edge project. Unfortunately, when these researchers left the laboratory to attend a conference, a terrible event occurred: the building janitor threw out all of their research materials. This disaster was so monumental and devastating that both young men had mental breakdowns. The white student committed suicide. Cowans quit medical school and took a job with IBM. The janitor who precipitated the devastating tragedy was not fired.

I listened and reflected on this story. Could this entire event have been an accident? Was it intentional? Who's to say? However, years later, I had a similar experience as a college instructor. Though not as devastating, the sting still serves as a warning to heed reality. Haters lurked everywhere. Life was unfair. In Nebraska I still was a virgin.

CHAPTER 18

PAIN IS GAIN

1970] At one of the Holy Roller Churches I attended in Indianapolis, were three fellows who had been recently released from incarceration. These men were self-taught, self-proclaimed gospel preachers. They had not graduated from high school, let alone college, and were of the "Howling Seminary" style of preaching. Their skills included the ability to yell and preach in high pitched screeches. They parroted bible passages and popular phrases originating from Dr. Martin Luther King, Jr. or other role models. "Hallelujiah, I... I... I... I have a DREAMMMMM! Yeeesss sahhh!" This was similar to what I had seen in Nebraska Pentecostal churches.

However, I was happily distracted by local church work, music, participating in theatrical productions and choirs, and coaching basketball and baseball as part of my work-study scholarship duties. It was doing this that set me up for an accident that would have a deep affect my future intimate relationships.

Each afternoon, after classes at CTS, I dutifully headed for the park. The Eli Lilly Pharmaceutical plant was directly across the street, and some days, the chemical stench was so horrible, it was hard to breathe. I was the coach for one of the city's youth teams, where I worked with the only with eight-to-twelve-year-old Appalachian white kids. I enjoyed teaching them the fundamentals of the sport. It was dealing with overbearing parents during games that was frustrating. I wanted the kids to relax and have fun, and this was difficult when parents insisted that their kids play above the level of their skills.

Some parents were even bullies, yelling, "If you don't hit that ball, I'm gonna beat your butt when we get home!" I felt sad for those kids and could relate to their struggles.

I often arrived at the park early, where Matt and Jimmy, two older boys who were not on my team, hung out. We often chatted about any topic that caught their curiosity. Matt had been raised in Indianapolis and was a slightly overweight tub of a kid—the stereotypical baseball catcher. Jimmy, his best friend, was from Kentucky and spoke with a slight stutter.

Both boys enjoyed talking about sports and their respective sports heroes. They eventually confided that I was the first black person they had ever talked to who didn't want to fight them. What had started out as a few short teaching moments of life and baseball, turned into several painful months of ball-bursting hell.

One day, Matt, the more talkative kid, was curious about continuing his education after high school and asked, "You majored in speech at the university, right?"

"That's right. I loved it. Speech is fun," I said.

"Ugh, I hate giving speeches. Why are you taking classes at the seminary? You gonna be a preacher or something?"

"Actually, I've already been doing some radio preaching on the campus FM station," I confessed. They looked impressed.

"I don't know if my parents can afford to send me to college," Matt said.

"M-m-me neither. That's why I like baseball. I wanna earn money playing b-b-baseball," Jimmy added.

"Hey, Mr. Aaron, you wanna see the four different pitches Jimmy can throw?" Matt asked, excitement bubbling on his face.

"Four? Sure, no problem. Can he really throw four different ones?" I teased. Perhaps it was a mistake for me to agree, but I saw no harm in playing catch with these two sixteen-year-old. I took Matt's catcher's mitt and bent into the catcher's position. "Hey, batter, batter! Hey, batter, batter!" I chanted good-naturedly.

The ball Jimmy threw hit my glove with a loud pop. It really stung. That first pitch did not seem like it came from a teenager. I could only hope it had been a fluke and that the next pitch wouldn't be so forceful. "Hey, Jimmy, how old did you say you are?" I asked as I threw the ball back to him.

The young kid from Kentucky sheepishly smiled and stuttered back, "You kn-kn-know. I t-t-told you: shixteen." With that, he made his slow wind-up, body curled, one knee high, the other planted. The ball came at me hard, hissing like a hot meteor.

This time, my reflexes were slow to catch it, and the ball flew just inches away from the leather glove. Then, a sudden shock of pain jolted my body. It felt like my genitals had been smacked by a hammer and then clamped in a vicious vice grip. I groaned and dropped to my knees.

Matt, standing nearby, was concerned. "Mr. Aaron, are you okay? Was that too fast?"

Jimmy triumphantly shouted from further away, "H-h-he can't catch my s-s-htuff.!" "Jimmy, he's hurt. Look what you did!" Matt accused his friend.

The young pitcher came closer. I slowly tried to straighten up. "Aww, m-m-man, I'm shorry," Jimmy mumbled. "That was just some junk I threw. Was trying throw a knuckler. Didn't you wear a cup? W-w-w-we always play hardball wearing a cup. Y-y-you know." I could not be sure whether I had detected a mischievous twinkle in his blue eyes, and a half-hidden smirk.

"Yeah, Mr. Aaron. You're a college graduate. You should know to wear a cup playing baseball," Matt added.

Finally catching my breath, I tried to make light of the situation. "Well, we normally just play softball here. And I don't play, I just yell at the kids. But I gotta tell you, that ball you threw sure hit my junk. Damn, it was fast! That's enough for me. Here, Matt, take your mitt back. I'm done. I'll just watch you guys."

It was very difficult not showing how much pain I was in. I took a while getting comfortable on a metal bench. Shortly afterwards, I coached the younger kids through a few drills as they played a scrimmage game. Time crawled tortuously slow. The pain did not start to subside until later that evening. Thankfully, my penis was still intact. I kept regularly checking my sex organs. It would have been a shame to never have been with a girl and forced to become a eunuch.

I assumed the pain would go away entirely within a few days, but it did not. A few days later, my Canadian co-worker, Laurene, invited me to her apartment for dinner after work.

There was nothing romantic between us. She was happily engaged to be married. However, at her apartment, I met her roommate, a foxy, scantily clothed white girl who looked like a runway model. Her tall, shapely body left a seductive trail of perfume in its wake, and her blouse "accidently" flared open occasionally as she applied the finishing touches to her makeup before heading out for her own evening date.

By the time she left, my penis was well past the hard-on stage, and I was in a great deal of pain. I discretely excused myself to the restroom. There was a wet stain of fluid on my underwear, and my swollen scrotum sack hung between my legs like a huge, brown, hairy mango. I was horrified and started to worry again about my sexual future.

However, things seemed okay the next morning. After choir rehearsal that day, as Anivo and I chatted and practiced French kissing in the car, my penis hardened again. She had never allowed my hands to venture beyond her breasts. Thus, I needn't have worried about her rubbing my genitals, which would have surely caused more swelling and pain.

Maybe this was a blessing in disguise. I would not be tempted to aggressively pursue any romantic liaisons in my painful physical state. I dismissed the notion of seeking medical attention altogether, as I did not trust doctors. I assumed things would get better on their own in time. I just had to be patient.

Near the end of the summer, I decided to visit my family in California before starting the fall term. Maybe I would get lucky out West. After all, lifestyles were quite different there than in the Midwest. I was starting to notice that the pain and swelling in my groin increased dramatically immediately after eating dinner. The less I ate, the less my scrotum swelled.

Indianapolis and I had not been a good fit, but back home in San Bernardino, there was still tension. Daily church attendance was still mandatory. This made me realize that I would never be comfortable continuing this fruitless routine. There was virtually no time for any leisure activities unless you had a solid excuse. Missing any church service was risky like playing hooky from school.

CHAPTER 19

LAND OF LINCOLN

The night our long journey ended we drove wearily into the city of Bloomington, Illinois.** Crossing the state line had been highlighted by foreboding signs. Unlike the end to the Children of Israel's happy crossing of the Red Sea, the "Welcome to Illinois, Entering the Land of Lincoln" sign, was misleading. The night sky was blanketed with flying locust. The surreal scene of insects shading each streetlight to a dim glow was weird. Also, our assigned apartment was on Locus Street. This should have warned us this part of USA was not the promised land. I had no idea this was a place without promise. My successful completion of my masters' degree in Communication Sciences suggested the opposite. The realities of the old southern ways, I assumed had long died, suddenly confronted me as soon as the Bloomington city administrators hired me months before graduation. I became the first Human Relations Officer, and also the first Black employee who was not a policeman, or parking Meter-Maid.

Bloomington had had four Black cops, but one had recently quit the force. There was trouble in the Land of Lincoln. Big trouble.

The after a first week on the job, trying to organize for community visibility and complaint processing, an invitation came from the city Mayor. I scheduled a meeting and soon stood in his office. The Mayor did not invite me to sit down. It was clear the meeting would be short, as he also remained standing. I assumed that our meeting would be small chit-chat get to know you kind of thing. Our meeting was short. His words also terse and to the point, although he kept staring down at papers on his desk.

"Young man," he said, "I been hearin' all day long on the radio that you're from the West... California..." I smile and quickly interjected my affirmation. "Yes, this is correct." He glanced up, shooting sharp steely gray eyes at me, and looked down again. The few black and gray hair strands sparsely covered his shiny dome. His spectacles miraculously remained perched on nose end. "Well. I just gonna tell you this. I am Mayor here. And down here...", there was a long pause as he searched for the right words, then he continued "we do things differently. You go on now. Have a nice day."

The man sat down and resumed his paper shuffling and signature signing. Not more than a time beat had passed when his secretary rushed into the office handing him another stack of forms for signatures. I had been dismissed. But this was only the start of my trail and tribulations in the human relations arena.

Soon after my wife, VJ, had become employed, she quickly secured the position as Director of the Sunny Side Day Care Center. Affirmative Action fallout was everywhere. Housing problems; Union Employment issues; School parent teacher conflicts, and housing law violations took more than nine to five attention. Most pressing in the news was conflicts between Black citizens and police, as well as, racial tensions within the police department. There were meetings on top of meeting, day and late at nights. Soon my wife and I were at loggerheads. VJ was not going to take these days and nights of my anxiety in silence.

"Just tell me, what do you think you can really do?" Her voice, while not loud, was firm and accusative.

First, I tried to be noncombative. "What do you mean? I don't know what you're trying to say." VJ would have none of my evasiveness. This was a continuation of earlier discussions. She came at me full bore. "You KNOW what I mean. Prejudice is prejudice. Racism is racism. White people have not changed over two hundred years. Your little office is not going to change the system."

"Well, are you blaming me for trying to be part of solution? People need help, don't you agree?" Hearing this VJ's voice raised an octave. "You are not Jesus Christ! Why waste your time working overtime when you could and should be relaxing at home? That makes no sense."

"Honey... Baby...Love! I enjoy this job, the challenge. It really makes me feel alive doing something meaningful. Every day is a new with fresh challenges. A lot more than stuck in rooms teaching students who really could care less about the outside world."

We had been going round and round on the issues regarding change agents roles and time spent on work related problems while at home or away from home. I thought by now we were closer together when it came to the fight for equality in as many arenas possible. I was mistaken.

This was not the only glitz in trying to plant roots in the lower half of Illinois. The city administrators asserted efforts to interfere with human rights complaint processing. I stubbornly refused to play political games with case related evidence and legal procedures. The atmosphere of drama increased like movie scenarios. The climax appeared when my expected salary increased stalled. One month, then from two to three months. Not did our finances suffer, our marriage also went down the tubes. Divorce although not unfriendly was inevitable. I also resigned from my human relations position. This was the first time I also had to declare bankruptcy.

During the interim, while working as a car salesman, my interest in equal rights work had not died. With the intention of applying to law school, I had successfully passed the law school, LSAT, examination. As luck would have it, a Student stipend was offered by university of Pittsburgh's law school. The Speech Communications department on the same campus also offered me a Teaching Fellowship. With much enthusiasm I headed east for more academic conditioning.

"Why do you want to come here? I'll ask you again. Why Pitt?"

The source of my interrogation was from a tall, wiry, bespectacled, Black man. His thick bushy dark mustache reminded me of Gaucho Marx. Comical, but dead serious. He stared at a copy of the same letter of invitation and admission to the law school. I knew that he was fishing for a different answer than the one I had given. I wanted tools useful for practical purposes. I tried to emphasis this goal.

"Like I said, my experience in human rights work revealed a serious need for citizens to become more aware of the law. I need skill in applying the law. I have found that citizens often do not know their legal rights. Worse, several White attorneys have privately said to me, sorry, although this or that case is solid, I cannot take it. Those respondents are my neighbors. We attend the same church. I have a family to feed. I live here."

Saying this I thought would motivate the law school Dean to admit me. This would mean a monthly stipend for books and accommodations as indicated before my arrival. But the dean was stalling. His next remarks would signal the direction of my future.

"Well… let me say this. I know the same person that you know. Pamela Rae. She's a white girl. So I really do not think you came to Pitt because you want to study law. You could have gone anywhere. I'll have to think about your answer. I'll let you know sometime next week. I'll look over this application again. There are many others who would love to get a shot to come here." He looked at me with owlish eyes through thick bifocal lens. After tight smiles and firm handshakes, I was out the door. I never went back.

*****

[1979] Pamela Rae (Scorpio), my second wife, had been trying to persuade me of the necessity of a vasectomy for a while, and my virility eventually became a serious point of contention between us.

We had just returned from our second Caribbean cruise, during which we seldom spent time together. Such trips served as mini-breaks-together from each other. And now, Pam wanted— needed—to talk. "Five years ago, I had my tubes tied. I knew I would never be a good mother, and I never wanted to have children. I would think that since you're from a large family, you wouldn't want a house full of kids. You really should get a vasectomy."

"I'm not going to have anyone cutting up my body. A vasectomy goes against nature," I argued.

"It makes sense to me. The population is getting out of control anyway."

"It makes sense to you, but this body is mine, not yours. That's a big difference," I said.

Beyond these arguments, Pam was a good sex partner. She loved sports and stayed informed about current events. I enjoyed having a female partner who was also a good sports- fan buddy. Tennis was the one sport I wanted to keep as my solo hobby, so she joined a ladies; rugby team to make up for deficient tennis skills. This proved to be fun for both of us, because the team asked me to serve as the team medic. She was also a staunch supporter of soon-to- be-President Jimmy Carter. It pleased me to know such a socially active white person.

Pam was tall, a natural blonde, big boned, and with a prominent hawkish nose and high cheek bones. Her steel blue eyes could be penetrating. She was bold, possessed a sharp tongue, and was fast-thinking and perceptive. I loved her emotional exuberance, but it came with a downside. She chain-smoked excessively— almost two packs a day, in fact. When she wasn't taking drags on cigarettes, she was smoking weed. She would follow up by relaxing with large amounts of late-night snacks, resulting in weight gain. I blamed the extreme stress on her profession as a diversity mediator consultant.

For me, being in this relationship clearly marked the end of my innocence. We had met at a human rights event in Atlanta, Georgia. After living together for a year, we decided to marry for the tax breaks and reliable sex. Initially, we were proud to be a pioneering interracial couple.

But I had ignored two pieces of sage advice: "Never marry for the wrong reasons" and "Keep away from those white girls." While I don't think we were wrong to promulgate the public image of racial unity, I had yet to realize getting married simply to make a political statement is not a good foundation for a marriage.

Eventually, we were quibbling over things both major and minor. Our attempts at communication would inevitably end in furious debates. We seemed to agree on virtually nothing. I was frustrated and angry. We were clearly both struggling. What is communication, really? In our case, it was blasting word bullets and phrase-slicing daggers.

Waiting in long lines to get gas for our automobile during the Iran oil crisis seemed to be prime time for explosive arguments. There was no peace even in our new Texas home of vaulted ceilings. I never got to have the last word, not even over my own body. The vasectomy issue soon roared to the surface and revealed our clashing values. I tried my best to be rational and communicate amicably with Pamela, but things always seemed to go awry.

For the next three years I taught in the Speech-Communications School. I also took graduate business courses and was particularly attracted to coursework in GISPIA's International studies on the same campus. Soon I had passed my Comprehensive Examination and could plough more time into dissertation research. I had by now already passed my first oral defense in Communication Studies.

Pam and I had married by now. I had never in a thousand years thought that I would be part of the interracial fringe. However, in my mind I deserved the right to choose whoever agreed to be joined with me in partnership. This was law. Doing this, the target on my back had increased in size. Perhaps both of us were subconsciously fatalistic. But the only thing mattering to me was that my partner was fiercely committed to the human rights fight. She was a competent desegregationist educator. Her work was part of a federal agency and her team travelled nationally holding intense sensitivity training workshops. Their job was emotionally grueling. This was the first time that I became a partaker of marijuana. Pam was a professional. She also smoked half of a pack of Salem Lights daily. She kept two small respirators handy because she was plagued by asthma attacks. We pitted the risks from vasectomies versus smoking. For a longtime we were stalemated. I hated cig smells.

When I received three new employment offers, we moved to Texas. Pam enrolled part-time in law school while employed in the city's Office of Human Rights. My new job was Associate Professor at TSU. Texas Southern University was a land grant school. The majority of the students African American and foreigners. Outside class clashes and politics would highlight my adventures in Texas. Maybe my journeys from Indiana, Illinois, and Pittsburgh had prepared me for what was soon to come.

CHAPTER 20

Teaching War Zones

" Hey man, you the teacher?" Louder voices from the brazen, restless students suggested they ran this classroom. They were outspoken and unafraid of authority figures.

"Brotherman, you ain't no teacher. You too young." "Yeah, you like us: just shucking and jiving. Hustling."

"What you gonna try to teach us that we don't know already? "Yeah, what you gonna teach us?"

I smiled and remained silent. The Pittsburgh classroom full of young black teenagers laughed. Many wore Pittsburgh Steelers or Pittsburgh Pirates sports paraphernalia. They were streetwise and heady in their own special knowledge. The sassy gum-chewing girls and gangster-wannabe boys in this high school social studies class on the verge of rebellion. And I was the substitute teacher.

I waited until the final bell rang and the last of the tardy walked in. One or two latecomers tried to slink in unnoticed. The chairs and desks in the room had previously been pushed away toward the walls, and the wooden floor visible in the center of the room was gouged and splintered. It was like this room was a war zone. I was filling-in for the regular teacher who, I was told, had been hospitalized suffering a heart attack while breaking up a classroom fight. The room windows had thick metal screens. There was no escape for either students or me the new teacher.

Now they were sizing me up, deciding what form their rebellion would take. They normally ignored substitutes. As the school Principal had handed me the room keys that morning, his only advice had been, "Just keep them in the room and out of the halls until after the second bell rings. Good luck." Clearly, he did not expect anything from me beyond babysitting the teenagers. There was no lesson plan for me to follow.

Before entering the main administrative office, I knew this assignment would be difficult. Signs everywhere shouted that this was more like an asylum or detention center than a place of learning. Muscular, black uniformed security guards were stationed at the ends of the long hallways. A thin haze of smoke hovered overhead just below the white fluorescent lights.

The unmistakable aroma of cannabis filled the air.

But what the principal didn't know was that I had seen worse school conditions in other states. In fact, I had even faced classes of inmates, incarcerated long-term for sordid crimes.

Prison is a place where people take the opportunity for any type of formal academic class as a welcome luxury and an opportunity not to be squandered. A hard life has taught many inmates the value of obtaining more information. These kids I now faced thought life was a picnic and that school was a prison. I would attempt to change their minds.

Setting my ring of classroom keys on the large teacher's desk, I began. "Alright class, how many of you know somebody who is in jail or has gone to prison? Raise your hand."

Suddenly there was silence. The students looked around nervously at one another. First one, then two surly-looking boys wearing baseball caps backwards and bulky gold chains raised their hands half-heartedly. They dropped their heads and slouched lower in their chairs. A murmur of assent and mumbled words punctuated the quiet room. A few more hands went up.

"Yeah, so what?" one boy asked, his voice hostile. "We all know about prison. I got an uncle who was inside for five years." His comment was immediately minimized by other students.

"Aww, dawg, that ain't nothing. Two of my brothers still inside. One for armed robbery.

The other for assault and battery. You know, some bullshit."

"I ain't afraid of serving time," someone shouted from the back of the room. "It's gonna be happening anyway. You know how The Man is. I gotta get me some paper, and he ain't be hiring, so I gotta do what I gotta do." A chorus of agreement ensued.

"Yeah, man. Word up. This high school trip is bogus. They ain't be giving out jobs after graduation. This is a waste," another added. A brief pause in discourse was my cue to assert my leverage for control.

I took the reins of the conversation. "Alright, so you think you're wasting time here?

You think jail time will improve your life? Are you saying that prison is a fun place to be?"

"Man, what you know 'bout it?" one of the previous speakers called out. "You just here slavin' away for The Man an' getting' chump change. I gonna get me some paper so I can enjoy life while I'm still young, man. May have to cap somebody's ass to do it, but it is what it is. My dad says life's a bitch."

"Yeah, man, at least in jail you get something to eat every day. And you don't need to go looking for no stupid job. Outside, some of us be lucky to eat at least once a day," another called out.

I heard these young people out and managed to steer the conversation toward making choices and bearing the consequences. I shared stories from past inmates I had taught. I told them about these men's regrets and the reality of being treated like dogs by guards. I told them stories of fellow inmates who preyed on each other like savages and how the simple wish for a peaceful night's sleep was impossible. I managed to control the class simply because they were all interested in each other's stories and curious about the new information I provided as an outsider. The class period went by quickly, and before I knew it, the class dismissal bell rang.

The students seemed reluctant to leave. There were stragglers, they lingered to ask questions or make comments they did not want others to hear.

I sat on the edge of the teacher's desk as the next group surged into the room. They were quieter than the first group. Perhaps word had gotten around the hallways that the new substitute teacher was serious about talking and listening to them. Each new class that filed in that day seemed hopeful, expectant, and curious about what lay in store for them. I had no discipline problems all day and even rewarded some particularly cooperative classes with their choice of favorite activities. By the end of the day, I was exhausted. I had learned that students wanted to be directly engaged. Maybe I was doing something right. Listening more, talking less.

As I was preparing to leave the school at the end of the day, I couldn't find the keys I had placed on the desk earlier. The principal told me not to worry about it, as I would not be requested to return. I was not surprised. Perhaps I was not the messenger the school administrator wanted around these students.

CHAPTER 21

Ocean of Soul

The campus of Texas Southern University offered me an opportunity to be closer to my own people. Initially, that felt good, but I needed to become more relaxed in an environment where few, if any, white faces could be seen. Maybe I really was an Oreo. Black outside but thoroughly brainwashed inside. Whatever I felt was a byproduct from immersion in totally White institutions for such a long time. While teaching at TSU, I had the pleasure of working with Dr. Thomas Freeman, and instructor of Congresswoman, Barbara Jordan. I also had spent many leisure hours working on my tennis game at the McGregor Park Tennis Center. My coach was John Wilkerson, also life-long coach for Zina Garrison and Lori McNeal, young black teenagers who would later rise high in the world professional tennis ranks.

At TSU, I had the honor to shake hands with Muhammad Ali when he visited to receive his honorary doctorate. To experience Ali's off-the-wall humor made that event had been a mental blast. Houston, Texas was an epicenter for the small community of Black movers and shakers. There were clear divisional lines between upper, middle, and lower economic statuses. Even, distinctions between spiritual adherents was emphasized by one particular campus professor. Bobby Mills had students marching around the campus perimeters chanting:

"These walls must come down! These walls must come down!" Professor Mills had published a book, Christianity: The Great

White Lie". One of his goals was to impress upon his learners of the racist tenets supported by Christian believers, and the fallacies inculcated by believers in superstitions. Many colleagues viewed Mills out of his mind. "That man's crazy! We can't believe where he gets such nonsense from!" However, I smiled and gave him my support feeling that I had finally found a kindred spirit. The following poem, "Fundamentally" I wrote and published around that time, reflected my views on the church-going robots we Blacks had been hoodwinked into becoming. I then wrote and published the poem:

FUNDAMENTALLY

Jesus in your bottle, let me take a sip

'til you and I together get ripped, ripped, ripped

On those who got no juice to make their rhythms flow

Those who got no mousse making hair stand
at the show.

Pour me some that wine just force it down my throat

ain't evil that I swallow like mainlining on some Coke.

Don't make me choke on prayers; don't make me
dance to songs

Don't make regurgitations quake from kneeling all
night long.

Your slight inebriation has me tripping in the mind

This measuring of the faithful through years has
made you blind

To the fact that Jesus is dead, Muhammad, and
Buddha too

But spirits from their peace beckons you

To PUT the bottle DOWN and be FREE!

CHAPTER 22

Romantic Optimism

After my stint in Pittsburgh I had ceased attending any church. For me it had been a relief to have not been affiliated with organized religion. Most of my leisure time had been spent travelling globally and doing battle on tennis courts. Yet, I felt there was something I could do as an attempt to lessen friction between competing religious denominations. I naively believed in the possibility of Christians businesses becoming less feudal, restrictive, and territorial. But in Houston, I felt suffocated in my marital relationship. I could no longer avoid making a decisive move. Three years into marriage it was clear to me that my relationship with Pam was unhealthy and needed to end. I detested being around smoking almost as much as hating being pushed to have a vasectomy. Our rationalized fires of romance had been shallow and fleeting. Lopsided reasoning had not been enough to preserve our relationship. We went to marriage counseling, but it only highlighted new reasons why we shouldn't stay together. I was tired of breathing in Pamela's secondhand cigarette smoke. I had quit smoking cannabis and no longer wanted to be around it. Plus, women of color were suddenly looking especially appealing. And yet, despite all of this, I couldn't seem to communicate my angst about our conflicting values.

We both became increasingly savagely blunt.

Finally, one night, our endless argument about getting a vasectomy came to a head. "Let's be civil about this," I said to

Pam, "You made your decision about your body. Now at least be civil while I stand by my decision. I'm just not comfortable with the idea."

"Oh yeah, we'll be 'civil' about this, all right. We'll be so civil that from now on, you can talk to my L-A-W-Y-E-R, okay? Is that clear? You better sleep elsewhere tonight. Get your things out of the house before the weekend, because I really want to keep being 'civil' as you call it."

There was a long silence in the room. The atmosphere felt heavy and thick with the hot charges of emotional conflict. I stared blankly off into space, lost in a thousand thoughts. I had not moved. Pam soon broke the quiet with her angry, cutting sarcasm. "After all, you never know what might happen when you're asleep. Maybe the spirit of Kathy Bates or Jack the Ripper will become imbued in my body. Unpleasant things might happen. You never know. Just like how I didn't know you were such a spineless shit until now."

I didn't know how to respond, but I was not going to be ordered out of my own house. Pam wasn't done just yet. She plowed on: "Fuck you and your merry ride to hell! I'll give you a list of some pretty female lawyers, too, so you can try to get your, lonely pecker wet with other experiences. You always were a sucker for a pretty face! But, mark my words: we're going to court with this, buster, so you'd better get your sorry ass ready. Good night."

With that, Pam stubbed out the unfinished portion of her smoldering cigarette. She turned away, heading off to the bedroom, stopped and turned halfway there. "Oh, and by the way, get out by the end of the week or else you might just lose that wandering cock of yours. Be warned."

I finally found my voice. "I'm not going anywhere! So, you do what you're going to do, and see what happens! These could be the last moment for you to suck on those cancer sticks you love so much!" That was the last time we saw each other of spoke. She was gone within the hour.

I headed to divorce court without hesitation, and soon moved back to Illinois to be in middle America, a better environment of suburban Chicago. By the time I reached Illinois, I had gone completely insane and fallen head over heels in love. Unknown to me, though, I had jumped from the frying pan into the fire.

*****

Changing beds again, moving into a new locality up North was a breath of fresh air, but also costly. I was back in Illinois, the land of Lincoln, further north and closer to Chicago. I had lost the house in Texas. Neither one of us wanted to deal with the business related to it. I was unemployed full-time for almost four months. Substitute teaching barely kept me in a new budding romance. This really took a mental toll on me. Eventually, I had to declare bankruptcy again.

I had sent at least fifty resumes and had ten job interviews. One interview was at David C. Cook's Publishing house for a management position. This business was located directly across from our home at the corner of Grove Street and Slade Avenue. Cook's designed and distributed Christian religious materials nationwide. In my youth these were the only study materials we had used for Sunday School lessons. The blue-eyed white Jesus was consistent on cards and teaching books. During a few months living at Slade Avenue I had noticed a group of black and brown women worked in the small cafeteria building a few yards away from the main sprawling office building. Venturing inside one day for lunch I learned these were the only minority workers employed at Cooks. When I told them of my intentions to have a chat with the owner in a few days, they looked at me as if I had lost my mind. The outcome of the eventual interview did occur. Unfortunately, Mr. Cook did not hire my services. I was not surprised.

Full Moon Biggi (Virgo) Brigitte Marianna became my third wife. By her appearance alone she quickly had me wrapped around her fingers. She was a part-time model and fulltime college teacher. Her thick German accent was exotic and compelling. Even before we married, colleagues at work noticed a big change in me. "Man, what's going with you?" a tennis friend asked one day.

"What are you talking about?"

"Look at you. You've been coming in to work with a big smile all over your face lately.

You're practically grinning from ear to ear," he said.

"Oh, you're right about that. This have a new girl, and we might get married. She is really hot!"

"What? A wife? Aren't you and Pam still married? When did all of this happen?" "It's long story, but Pam and I really just hooked up for the tax breaks. It was just a business deal, really, and now we've agreed to go our separate ways." This was a highly sterilized version of the truth, but it still was technically the truth.

I was hooked on Brigitte Mariana. I thought I had won a grand prize perhaps because of her physical appearance, love for tennis, and world travel. Her frequent moonlighting as a professional model..... My new soon-to-be wife was European and of medium height. She had long blonde hair, steel-gray eyes, an infectious smile, and a hearty laugh. She looked like the stereotypical trophy wife, and I was intrigued by her foreign accent, which turned on and off, cushioning her occasional jabs of sarcasm with humor. We were both speech teachers, so we shared our professional interests. Everything about her seemed exotic and different. I was smitten.

I didn't realize it yet, but like Pam, Brigitte, was an avid feminist and the issue of birth control would become important but different, she was attention starved. Or maybe she had become addicted to leers from men who desired at her modeling gigs. I tried to ignore her overtly flirtatious behavior toward complete strangers. She frequently said in a comedic voice: "I know *zees eez* true... I'm beautiful... everybody *vants* to *fawk* me!"

At first, I found this funny. However, after we passed the four-year mark, I could see that this was a badge of honor to her. Being seen as sexually desirable to all was essential to her being. Sadly, like clockwork, during each full moon period she ranted and raved.

I renamed her Full Moon Brigitte, because shortly after our marriage, I noticed a strange relationship between the moon and her mental disposition. Every month, when the moon reached perfect fullness, she would rage about anything and everything. All men were animals was her theme. Even before the earth's moon was completely round, she was prone to outrageous tantrums and mood swings. Apparently, she had been damaged by something from her past.

Two cats Full Moon Biggi owned had full range of the house. This added to my physical discomfort. At night, my allergies invariably flared up, and breathing became difficult without taking some form of medicine. Yet I stubbornly believed that our so-called 'paradise' could magically survive.

Together, we enjoyed antique-hunting adventures across Canada and the United States. I became addicted to collecting Black Americana memorabilia. These historic relics taught me a great deal about how negative racial stereotypes persisted. The marketing of demeaning folk art, paintings, sculptures, advertising, and sheet music, denigrating blacks, were evidence that black Americans have long been commercially objectified negatively. Clearly, over the years, this pattern of conditioning white mentalities had effectively objectified and denigrated blacks.

On a visit to Chicago, one reality of my relationship with Full Moon Biggi crystalized in an uncomfortable way: we were targets. As we drove through the city, an unmarked police car flashing a revolving blue light suddenly blocked our car, and two white men sprang out of it and demanded I exit my vehicle. One of the men flashed a gold-plated badge. Apparently, they were undercover detectives. I followed his instructions calmly, but he roughly spun me around, kicked my feet wide apart, shoving me against the car, and frisked me. The other man opened the car door on Full Moon Brigitte's side, grabbed her purse to dump contents onto her lap.

I was interrogated: "Are you carrying any weapons?"

"No, sir. What's the problem, officer?"

"Show your license and registration."

Meanwhile, the other man continued rifling through my wife's purse. He scrutinized each object.

Finally, the officer beside me explained: "We stopped you because there's been a robbery in the area, and you fit the description: a mixed couple driving a black two-door Chrysler. Sorry about that. Have a good day."

Just as quickly as they appeared, they were gone. Our car had been searched, my wife's purse thoroughly sifted through, and I had been frisked. A crowd at the corner bus stop continued to stare as we composed ourselves.

As we got back in the car Full Moon Brigitte fumed. She had not been accustomed to repeated encounters with the police. Her German accent thickened in anger: "*Z'is eez* ridiculous!"

"You got that right."

"*Vy* didn't you do *som'zing*? You were quiet. 'Yes, sir. No, sir.' Such a coward. You could have at least said *som' zing!*" she said.

"Listen, all they need is an excuse to take me into the station. It's best to just cooperate."

She was silent a moment then said, "Still, you should have said *som'zing*. Protest, *dammeet!*"

"I will," I promised. "I'm going to call the station and make an official complaint. I have the name and badge number of one of those guys. That's the best course."

That seemed to placate her.

The next day, I called in our complaint, providing details of the event.

"Yes, we've heard about those two detectives," the officer I spoke to said. "This isn't the first time a citizen has lodged a report against them."

Clearly, we were targets. This was nothing new to me, but Brigette was not used to it and found it distressing. It took some time for the shock of the Chicago police fiasco to wear off for her.

A few months later, Full Moon Brigitte accused me of stealing from the school speech team travel fund. According to her, she left the money somewhere in her office and now it was missing. I had no idea of this problem until she accused me of being the culprit. Blindsided by her accusation, I felt deeply wounded. She never apologized, and I realized we had more than trust issues to be concerned about.

One night, I received a call late in the evening. We had just rented a booth in the town's antique mall, and Brigitte had spent the evening there, painting and decorating. She called me from there, hysterical. "There's someone here!"

"Huh?"

"There's someone here in the rear of the store. I'm scared. There isn't supposed to be anyone here but me! Please come quickly! Hurry!"

"Okay, have you called the police?" "Yes! Just hurry up and get here!" "I'm coming!"

I reached the State Street Mall in about five or six minutes of reckless driving. My wife's car sat alone in the parking lot outside the collection of small antique shops. Everything was dark inside except for the front lobby lights. I knocked on the door, and in a few seconds, Full Moon Brigitte appeared.

"Are you okay?" I asked.

"No, that's why I called you. Will you look in the back and see if anyone's there?" "Okay, wait at our shop booth."

With my small floodlight in one hand and my hammer in the other, I started my search. Slowly proceeding to the rear of the store, I checked inside each booth. There was nothing and no place for anyone to hide.

Suddenly, I heard noises coming from the front of the store. Stepping back into the main aisle, I started to retrace my steps. Without warning, a group of flashing lights came directly at me. "Hey, you! Put your hands up!" a voice barked. The flashlights blinded me, and I froze, stunned by what was happening. "Drop your weapon!" the voice repeated.

The next thing I knew, three guns were pointed at me from different directions. The voices were those of policemen. My hammer clanked on the floor. One voice demanded, "What are you doing here?"

In the background, I heard my wife's familiar laugh. "Oh, it's okay. That's my husband.

Ha ha ha!"

All I could think about was that this had been a close call. Perhaps even a planned set- up. My wife had demonstrated a lack of trust toward me in the past. Now, I had a deeper lack of trust toward her. It was clear that she had not alerted the police that I was in the back searching for the supposed intruder. The officers had to pass our booth—and her—before reaching me. Apparently, I still appeared cowardly to Full Moon Brigitte. I was so deeply in love with her, my prized trophy, that I had lost my self-respect. These became dark times in our marriage. My allergy to her cats worsened.

Full Moon Brigitte spouted anti-male vitriol constantly, and my response to it was virtual silence. I knew she egged me on to react emotionally. I was reluctant to take her bait. Occasionally, I offered feeble defenses of my gender and stubbornly claimed to be different from other men. I just wanted to preserve our legally sanctioned public union. The wild sex hopefully would continue. But her constant bickering, complaining about our male-dominated society, and verbal castrations only got worse with time. I repeatedly asked her why she had married me: "Tell me, if men are so awful, why on earth are we together? Why didn't you marry a woman?" Full Moon Brigitte laughed. "I can't see myself rubbing against a woman, boobs-to-boobs. That's just silly. The truth is, I thought you had a lot of money when I saw your house in Texas."

"Oh, I see. Then you admit to just being a gold digger? Did you ever love me?"

"Don't be such a romantic. A woman must use her assets. My mother always said a girl won't have her looks forever. I did what I had to do."

I was stunned. The reality was our relationship had been built on materialism and sex. I had been blinded by idealized romance and social image. Conditioned by media. Thinking I had achieved a reward, I had been willing to do almost anything that preserved the status quo. This was not a win-win situation. The spell was broken. I had to face the fact that Full Moon Biggi had a whole host of unbearable baggage.

One day not long after this, we were in the shower together, and she took out her diaphragm and placed it on my head.

I looked at her in surprise. This act came totally out of the blue, without preamble or provocation. "What are you doing? You think this is funny?" I asked, confused.

"Yeah. It suites you. If you don't like it, hit me. Go ahead! Hit me!" When I didn't move, she slapped my face. "You are really a coward!" she spat.

She raised her hand, preparing to strike again, but this time I grabbed both of her wrists firmly. Her eyes burned fiercely like hot pokers. She seemed possessed, yet I determined calmed her down. "Hold on! Hold on! What is your problem?" I said. "You know I don't hit women! You need to relax. *Relax*!"

"Let go of me you, coward! Let me go… *nigger*!!!" she screamed.

At that moment, I knew we were done. I let go of her and backed away without saying another word. Her insults and disrespect had crossed the point of no return. I would do whatever necessary to extract myself from this hell. Hanging on to this relationship was foolish. For this, I had virtually forsaken tennis, running, and writing as outlets. My life had been totally hers to use. I felt emasculated. I had foolishly become her voluntary slave. This anesthetized relationship was doomed.

The final straw came two days later—two days in which Brigitte had been completely absent. She telephoned and simply said, "I just had an abortion. I didn't want to discuss it with you." Our marital charade was over. Our so-called love had been entirely one-sided. Our 'paradise' together had turned into bondage and hell, and I could only blame myself.

*****

A year before my dad passed, I received an unexpected package. It was a gift of a new adult size baseball glove. He had always known of my romantic attachment to this game. A small note with his initials said, "This is for you. Enjoy the game!"

I smiled, and my eyes became moist. This was the type of odd thing I did that made me ignore his harmful behaviors. I knew this was a symbol of his love and an oblique apology. I needed to forgive the past and try to overlook our vast differences. For the first time, I invited my parents to our home. In all honesty, however, it would be extremely difficult for me to sit in any church again. I was done with phony posturizing.

CHAPTER 23

Clay Pigeons

A single, blind bullet came from an unknown origin point. It crashed through the thin walls of the storefront church where the fundamentalist cult members met. The worshippers became unusually still and quiet, and then my Aunt Lila slowly slumped forward. She died a few minutes later. From that moment on, guns and bullets were symbols of the Devil in our family. God sent messages that my parents couldn't stop repeating:

"The Devil is busy."

"God needs messengers like us to keep the enemy at bay."

I never told my parents, but from that day forth, I wanted to be a diplomat, a peacemaker. I could no longer ignore the wars between races, political groups, and countries. I thought it strange that we black church folk sang about being "soldiers" in the "Army of the Lord." Yet, most did not behave in ways that their words logically implied.

When it came to education, their actions also did not match their words. I was often beaten for getting bad grades, and yet when I was succeeding in school and setting my sights on a college degree, my parents said, "You shouldn't be striving for such worldly goals. You spend too much time with those books. That's Idolatry, worshipping man's ideas. It's not what the Lord wants for you. You should be like your father."

My father was a storehouse of mixed messages: do hard manual labor or pursue higher education; spend a part of each in church and ignore financial gain. At a young age, together we visited the campus of UCLA to watch the professional Los Angeles Rams football practice. As we passed a bulletin board with a list of job descriptions in one of the buildings, he made a point being explicit that I studied posted salary scales. "See this? Do you see this?" he repeated. "Six figures. Six figures!"

"Uh, huh. Yes, sir," I said, apprehensively, trying to be polite and remain on his good side. I did not want him to call me a knuckle head and box my ears.

"Do you know what this is?"

"No, sir."

"Six figures! Look at that: six figures! Count them." I squinted and looked closer at the spot where he was jabbing his calloused finger. He lifted the bottom of the posted announcement closer to my curious eyes. "Those are salaries, mister! This is what you should be making when you get through school. You are worth your weight in gold. Remember that."

Despite these early ambitions for me, my father's own prospects for job advancement turned bleak over time. Discriminatory setbacks disillusioned him, and with each vocational obstacle he faced, my father slid deeper into Pentecostalism and became more and more extreme in his parental, as well as spiritual, views. He started having wild nightmares and often woke screaming angrily and crying. He spoke in tongues and thrashed about in our living room.

When our family moved away from the comfort and security of south-central Los Angeles, I was exposed to new environments and extreme social conflicts. They set the stage for clashing values and behaviors regarding cultural harmony and equality. My goal to achieve academic and social success in high school was repeatedly blocked by parental dictums. Dad had changed his views regarding six figure salaries for me to have as a goal.

Problems with discrimination and internal family conflict added to the stress I was under, and it became increasingly clear that I needed to unshackle myself from my immediate family. Yet even as I did so, the church of my childhood remained a stable entity in my life as I bucked against contradictory demands. However, I eventually reached a turning point in my faith. I recognized confusing conflicts in various Pentecostal churches. My year in seminary had proven to be a disappointment and the catalyst for spiritual change.

While attending seminary in Indiana, Pentecostal church members often warned me, "Blacks who work for The Man commit an unforgivable sin."

Later, wearing the hat of 'teacher,' I was mocked by some of siblings and church members alike:

"If you're so smart, why ain't you rich? You think you're better than us, that's all.

"All that time you spend studying man-made theories should be devoted to God's holy word instead."

This clashed with my early dreams of being a nontraditional diplomat, a cultural representative of Americans. I continued to carefully guard my secret ambitions. Silence and determination were practical strategies.

Realities of academia, combined with entrenched racist attitudes on both sides of the cultural, were toughening experiences. My failed mixed marriages, and highly questionable communication skills were also critical intangibles. Over the years, the relative safety of classrooms, local communities, and experimental television programs afforded me growth opportunities. By not remaining encapsulated I embraced my role as an informal international diplomat. I simply could not see the sense of neither racial nor religious bigotry. Putting myself on the line, sticking out my own neck, took even more courage than staying at home in the USA.

*****

The aftermath of my aunt's death was numbing. The day of Aunt Lila Glenn's funeral was unforgettable. The ceremony was held inside an old renovated theater, which was now the Home Assembly Pentecostal Church. I loitered outside the church auditorium. At seven years old, I was deemed too young to see the deceased body displayed within. A sleek, black limousine stopped in front of the building. As a tall, barrel-chested, muscular man stepped from the backseat, the adult onlookers gasped and suddenly became attentive. The man was Roy Glenn, son of my Aunt Lela Glenn. His skin was a burnt-vanilla color, and he sported a neatly trimmed mustache. His bearing and posture were regal. Without a word, he solemnly marched into the cramped auditorium of mourners for the formal viewing of his dead mother.

Roy Glenn, my cousin, gained fame and notoriety for being one of the first male ethnic television and movie actors in Hollywood. His deep, authoritative voice and no-nonsense attitude drew respect and attention. Not only did he play countless butler roles, but also the father of Sidney Portier in the movie classic, *Guess Who's Coming to Dinner*. He was a trailblazer. I was tongue-tied. I couldn't even say hello to him. My past conditioning dutifully embraced the notion that children should be seen and not heard.

During the good years, I loved listening to my mother sing at home. On quiet afternoons, she practiced arias and love songs for weddings, but after many pregnancies, she sang less and less.

She often advised me to be more observant and less trusting, and while this was probably true, I had long since observed how adamant my mother, of mixed Cherokee and African descent, was against guns. Barely concealing moist eyes, she often reminded me, "Only murderous hearts own guns." As a child, I naively attributed her tears to the Los Angeles smog stinging her eyes. Gun-wielding white settlers had pushed her Native American ancestors to the brink of destruction in their greed for land. Gun-wielding whites in the South made life a living hell for black sharecroppers. The forces that had laid her people low for generations had done so with guns.

Any topics related to guns could easily push my mother's emotional buttons, resulting in a fit of anger. She did not allow guns in our house, and so my dad kept his carbine rifle from his military-service days at his buddy's domicile.

Growing up, playing Cowboys and Indians with my next-door neighbor was frowned upon, in part because we used toy guns. My friend, Little Tony, had two silver six-shooters with white leather holsters. One day, Little Tony let me use one of his toy guns while playing. My mother spanked me for bringing it inside our house. After this, I sneakily created toy guns out of scrap wood or branches.

Our family spent many hours attending church prayer meetings. I said the name Jesus so often I almost forgot my own. Jesus was mentioned in almost every other sentence in our house. Perhaps our daily attendance helped my parents forget the dreadful present and the difficult past. However, this church attendance almost came to a complete halt when my Aunt Lila died from a gunshot wound. As she sat in church one Sunday, a stray bullet from a pool hall argument across the street killed her. The deadly projectile went through her left eye and ploughed into the church's wooden pulpit. After this tragedy, it was difficult for me to enter a church building. Thoughts of being a sitting duck, haunted and evoked feelings of panic and mental angst.

Sixty years later I stood in a different type congregation. There, people came with a special reverence. Rituals were short and personalized: choice of weapons, ammunition, ear plugs, eye guards. We were worshippers of the holy gun. There was no long sermon, only short cautionary reminders. The indoor shooting range felt cool and serious, like a funeral parlor. I had to wade through spent brass bullet casings around my feet.

The periodic staccato sounds of distant gunshots were disturbing, yet poetic the silence. This was heavy metal music with distinctive meanings. Absent were angelic choirs, loud prayers, or the scents of erotic perfume. Instead, a strong aroma of acidic ammonia and burnt metal mixed with firecrackers stung my nostrils. A strong current from the air conditioner made one target sway like a kite in the breeze.

I steadied myself, eyes glued on the red laser pointer in the gun scope. This was our solemn sanctuary where we prepared for a crazy world. My forefinger lightly touched the trigger.

Pop! Pop! Pop!

On the distant paper target, three holes appeared without my permission. Each gun I held seemed to have lives of their own.

Pop! Pop! Pop!

The metallic sounds of brass casings zipped past my head before clinking on the concrete floor. A puff of smoke appeared at the end of the barrel. The scent of acidic burning ammonia enveloped the room. I thought of sage. These guns almost fired at will, vomiting forth three shots with the slightest touch. Their explosions startled me despite the ear plugs I wore beneath ear muffler cups clamped on my head.

My instructor, muscular and full of pumped enthusiasm, only reinforced my feeling of being beyond middle-aged. He praised my shooting skills, saying, "You're a natural-born sniper!" All three of my targets had holes tight in the kill zones. "You really nailed that sonofa bitch! He ain't gonna mess with you! You want to shoot some more rounds?"

The large paper targets I blasted were razzed where my bullets repeatedly penetrated them, but their human shapes lacked anything like blood oozing from metal-torn flesh. And this was no festive carnival atmosphere. There were no stuffed toy rewards for accuracy.

My instructor informed me that these guns' triggers were calibrated "light," which explained why they were so very sensitive. The definition of "hair trigger" became obvious. These weapons spat out torrents of angry lead destruction with the barest touch. They were holy toys for adult believers. Historically, those who knew the gospel of peace used tools like these to civilize the so-called "savage" American Indians—my mother's people.

This Sunday marked the first time I ever fired live ammunition. My mother's advice to be less trusting was stronger in my mind. Being older I was also more observant. I still had love in my heart, just smaller degrees of hope.

Uncle Glenn represented success that our family silently envied. Unfortunately, the constant contact had ceased because my parents said the Glenn's were "Indian Givers". They had given us a long mahogany polished dining table. This object disappeared a week after our admiration. Dad grumbled that Uncle Glenn had refused to listen to dad preach about saving his soul. Our relatives were Indian Givers for taking that table away after giving it to our family. But mom continued to take me to Aunt Lila's house during the day. I do not think either Uncle Glenn or dad were aware of these meetings. Mom did things like that. She had a great compacity to love.

This love was reiterated when I left home to return to Nebraska after semester break.

Mom handed me a new fashionable tan winter jacket with matching brim hat. "Take this. You'll need it. I know it's cold back there. Don't tell your father." The gift was boxed carefully and a complete surprise. With moisture in my eyes I gave mom a hug. It was unusual for her to accept this kind of tactile behavior from me. My other sibling hung back and sheepishly waved. Dad had not spoken to me for several days. I knew he felt betrayed the fact that I had been serious about leaving him with the church load. I had broken my robotic state of mind.

*****

I steadied my gun's sight on the cartoonish sci-fi target inside the noisy firing range. The gun is God. The gun agitates. It symbolizes a level of power and awareness of reality. Walking into a forest of wild animals is foolish when you're armed with only faith in chants, sacred relics, and the unknown. We are the crazy ones who think we can survive on false traditions of goodwill. Trust must be earned. The long lists of consequences from broken promises keeps pulling the mentally stable off tight ropes of social stability. The prepared ninja endures.

CHAPTER 24

Rubberband Man

I stood on a street corner in New York City, distracted by a homeless woman giving a long oral soliloquy to empty spaces. I had watched her for several minutes, taking in the familiar way she nodded her head, twisted her neck, and raised her eyebrows. The shape of her head and mouth and the sound of her voice seemed weirdly familiar. No one was near and she was not using any technology I was certain.

Suddenly, her speech abruptly stopped, and our eyes locked. We stared at one another, and the gap between us seemed to grow smaller as we examined each others' facial features, eyes, head shapes, and skin tone. And there it was: the familiar expressive Vessup lips, chin, and jawline. The long crinkly hair. The half-hidden scowl. The puzzled furrow between the eyes. Despite the many years that have passed, I knew her.

Early in our youth I had teased Lollie mercilessly. I mocked her when she talked to invisible friends in her empty room. I even claimed to know one or two of her imaginary characters. Late at night I dangled a ghostlike figure made from patches of white handkerchief, and a large round marble tethered with black thread. This figure floated by her bedside while she tried to sleep. I made frightening voice until she would awaken to scream. By the time our mother appeared I had quietly slid on the slick wood floor back into my room. I was safe, but this naughty torment soon ended. One day I overheard my mother tell my sister, "If your brother keeps teasing you, just put a broom upside his head.

He will stop bothering you." Sure enough, one day after Lollie and I had stopped playing badminton, I teased her about her loss. She ran into the house and returned with a wood broom. I wasn't expecting this, but she smacked my head with the wood part of the broom then turned and ran crying into hour house. "He's going to hit me! Mommy! He's going to hit me!" The way she wailed and cried in terror brought my mother quickly to the scene. No excuse on my part was good enough to overcome the vocal plea mom had heard. Lollie's alarm sounds, and look of desperation was sufficient. I never bothered my sister again. We also stopped playing badminton games.

The look on her face changes from curiosity, to confusion, and then to recognition in an instant. Suddenly, she backed away. The woman I thought to be my long-lost sister turned and sprinted away, yelling, "Storyteller! Storyteller!"

I ran after her, shouting, "Wait, Lollie! Wait, I need to talk to you! Wait!" It was a lost cause. Age had caught up with me, and though Lollie was just five years younger, her years of living on the streets of New York had made her speedy. Her master's degree in speech rehabilitation had proven useless, just like this failed attempt at making contact. My so-called communication skills were no match for this sibling who still felt persecuted. Her need to run from any family members had not changed. I had been told she routinely fled at the sight of a relative or sibling.

In some ways, my sister reminded me of Aunt Firecracker Dottie, born and raised in the Bronx and Harlem. Dotty Vessup was my dad's youngest sister. She was small in stature, while the other eight siblings were tall, but Dottie made up for her size with a loud, boisterous, iron- edged voice. Her loud, wild pronouncements often startled listeners. She had a feisty, volcanic personality and was always ready to challenge anyone to a fight, whether it be with fist, rock, or knife.

A bottle of *Jim Beam* and her preferred *Johnnie Walker Black Label* helped Firecracker Dottie spill a few secrets. Her experience of being raped early in her youth by two of the Pentecostal ministers in New York fueled her anger. She recalled being molested by two different church leaders, both of whom later become church bishops. It was painful to hear her recount memories of so-called holy men probing her vagina, ruining her innocence. They told her they were 'spiritual messengers' and that "God wants us to help you feel good." She has nothing to do with any church these days. After drinking her fill and telling her secrets, she would either drift off to sleep or bolt from her apartment down the street for an imaginary appointment somewhere. No one ever knew where.

Aunt Dottie now hung on to shreds of weakened sanity. Her behaviors seemed downright schizophrenic to me. In the end, Aunt Dottie lived on the streets until a final hospitalization. She passed away soon after. I'm told she cursed non-stop in her final hours.

Authority figures—God, the police, politicians, church leaders—all had become damnable sources of delusions. And now my sister, Lollie, again had escaped our parents' clutches returning to run in the New York City streets. This could have been her way of escaping the demons from her past conditioning that still haunted. She seemed to have lost her mental balance in desperation to be free from earlier restraints.

CHAPTER 25

CONNECTIONS

Escape from home had been aided by looking beyond the North American borders. The worlds I found contained a wealth of knowledge, as well as, mentally freeing experiences. I needed relief from zombie-eyed Christian zealots and mind-numbing hypnotic gospel music. Special experiences make deep impressions on two sides of the cultural divide. What follows are episodes and personal bench marks. Outside or off the formal stages I had achieved greater degrees of participation and awareness.

Haiti. As part of a cruise to the Caribbean islands I was anxious to reach Haiti. While this involved a bit of island hopping I finally arrived. I chatted confidently blundering my poor French with the young kids tagging alongside generous tourist. Also, I searched for something special. A Voodoo doll. Our group had been mounted singularly on squawny, starved looking donkeys making our way up a steep crooked mountain path reaching the famed Citadel, some distance from the capitol city, **Porte O'Prince**. The Haitians had successfully won a singular victory over invaders fortified inside this mammoth stone structure. I overheard the kids joke in French about various tourists, especially the fat white couple passing out five-dollar bills to eager hands. This particular couple loudly kept repeating that they hailed form the Great State of Texas. It seemed a miracle that the overweight passengers did not fall off the animals as they waddled, rocked and swayed precariously side to side. Unfortunately, I found it difficult fitting in when accompanied by a loud group of obnoxious Americans. Arrogance tends to be a Western stereotype affirmed in those situations.

Two Haitian men were assigned to each donkey. One yanked at the animals' halter and mouth bit. The other man held the donkey by the tail and swatted its back as blood streaked and smeared the animal's hunches. Returning to the bottom of the mountain trail I hurried to inquire about buying a Voodoo doll. My interest in the spiritual practices had been ignited having heard of the Haitian's historic resistance to embracing Christianity. Seeing many vacate, burnt, decaying shells of churches was an indication that folk here had managed to cling to their own traditional worship practices.

"No Voodoo doll! No Voodoo doll here!" Two brown policemen in sharp creased khaki uniforms and official hats, rained blows upon the last vendor I had approached. Had they been following me? They continued beating him as they averted their stern eyes in my direction. I felt sorry for the man who had been the only person willing to take me to where, he said these dolls were located. I should have been more alert to the fact that some practices are deemed secret. I needed to be more careful. And who knows, maybe the vendor really was not going to be my "helper". Perhaps the police knew more about scams than I.

CUBA. The brief afternoon rain had stopped. Traveling alone, I had left the train for a temporary stay in, **Camaguey**, a small touristy town. There was a brilliant rainbow on the horizon and the resort hotel valet seemed reluctant to take my new leather garment bag. Retrieving it from the taxi he had thrown it to the ground in the hotel lobby with what seemed to me, unnecessary force. He was a light skinned Cuban displaying an attitude after I had been checked in. At my room, again the Valet tossed my polished leather luggage to the ground. I became more irritated.

"Hey there! Watch it! Don't handle my bag like that. Can you be more careful?" "What 'ya got in there, gold?" He snarled.

"Look, if anything is broken you're going to pay the damages."

Later I checked on my two bottles of Guatemalan rum. This liquor had recently been awarded a gold medal world competition. The rum was to be gifts to my Cuban friends. Luckily the glass bottles had not broken. However, I did need to change to a better room. The door lock did not work, the doorknob literally hung from its hole in the door. The air conditioning did not work. Managing to obtain another room equipped with functioning conveniences was easy. However, I was surprised that my room location was the property's rear perimeter, far from the central building. It was clear the resort facility was virtually uninhabited. Before checking out from this place I was blindsided, having been charged $40 USD for a cheap plastic thermos that had exploded. The retail cost for such a thermos was between $!0-15 USD. Apparently, the accident of exploding glass inside the container had been caused by the gas filled ice container after I ordered ice. The entire check-out routine found me in the role of ugly American. Subsequently, I had to walk to the train station.

The city of, **Santiago de Cuba**, was quite the opposite as people everywhere were generally of darker complexions. Social attitudes reflected more brotherhood camaraderie-like behaviors. As a black man in Cuba, I could fit-in easily by simply being silent. I even experienced no scrutiny when accompanied by a local. My friends would say, "Antonio, as long as you do not speak your spanish we will be fine. The vendors will only charge us Cuban prices, not foreign prices." I knew they were correct giving this advice, because Cubans speak a rapid Spanish lingo. It would have taken me years of immersion to reach this language acumen.

In **Havana**, I noticed that even some black group tour guides, had negative attitudes toward me when in the presence of white tourists. It seemed the same behavior that other white Cubans make toward black Cubans. A supercilious manner and sarcastic vocal tones, tight faced or sneering. Basically, unpleasant civil workers. As a paying visiting tourists I sometimes had the feeling that I was paying to be abused, not gracefully serviced. However, this, too, obviously depended on where you were, as well as, with whom. I also experienced the extreme end of pleasant acceptance in other parts of the island. It also, seemed that if and when you were identified as some type of official, treatment was off-the-charts high. Color did not matter.

One funny revelation came when I purchased batteries from a small local shop. The dusty shelves were virtually empty. The sparse products seemed crusted with grim and dirt. The batteries that I had purchased for my camera did not work. Who knows how long they had sat in that dimly lit store. Returning twenty minutes later with the dead batteries I asked for a refund. The shop keeper was astonished by my request.

"Satisfaction guarantee! What is this you're talking about? We know nothing about guarantee. No refund. You bought it, those batteries are yours!"

Luckily, I managed to capture good photograph shots of graffiti art, during three other visits years earlier. My participation in the group exhibition held at fort El Morro in Havana was successful. The biggest surprise in Cuba, was the absence of advertisements of various well-known name brand items. The only brand advertised in Cuba was patriotism and general governmental party line themes.

MEXICO. climbing historic pyramids in this country was fascinating, and I enjoyed delicious "Cerviches" on clean beaches for perfect relaxation. I became a collector of carved wooden, miniature puzzled toys of birds, and fantasy creatures in **Huatulco**. Improving my Spanish skills while participating in an immersion language program in **Cuernavaca**, "Land of Eternal Springs". This helped me build communication skills profitable for future undertakings.

Delicious food always satisfied my palate and stomach, especially "Mole" chocolate dishes. Perhaps, most exciting was sleeping on the Pacific coast beach at night, after romping nude with a friend at night under the brilliant starry skies.

I was astonished, visiting the city of **Cholula**, learning that 365 churches existed. Some say these edifices represent the freedom for people to have an option of worshipping inside a different church every day in a year. In my view, this went a long way toward maintaining superstitions. The preponderance of so many churches in one place is absolute proof of obvious effects from years of brainwashing the masses.

GUATEMALA. In this Central American region exists several volcanos. A few were active, and I ventured to climb one of the live mountains among the five I personally faced. On several occasions, the airport in **Guatemala**, the capitol city, had been closed due to volcanic ash *Volcan Picaya*, that clouded arriving and departing aircraft. I experienced several adventures challenging my physical and mental abilities. Mountain climbing can be a self-discovery ordeal. Completing those challenges made me feel euphoric and highly motivated to face normal challenges life presents. Being in an earthquake while watching a volcano in the dark night, several miles away, was a thrill and quite scary. The building structure swayed at least one foot without crumbling down. Talk about fear factor! This was the that! One cannot ignore the huge colorful fruit and vegetables. Tall cornstalks towered on hillsides. Vendors roasted corn along streets, and sold and fried bread. The dust trailed speeding chicken buses, loaded inside and on their roof tops. With other local passengers we have departed from the quaint touristy town of **Antigua**, for a two-hour mountain ride up steep, twisting roads. Our driver frequently challenged oncoming bus for right of way on narrow lanes. We had many close calls. Passengers prayed loudly while making signs of the cross on their panicked chests. These journeys were perilous.

A funny thing happened during my first trip to Guatemala. One bright day, on my first visit to Lake Atitlan, a group of my Spanish language school decided to venture from the town of **Quetzaltenango**, to **Panajachel**, up in another mountain region. I had taken a small boat taxi across the lake to the small town of **San Pedro**. This was a typical touristy town but smaller than "Pana", which served as a transportation hub to outer parts of Guatemala. On the way back, the taxi boat briefly stopped at a village called

San Juan. Decided to investigate this village of a different Mayan tribe than other villages around the lake, I disembarked. It would be two hours before the next boat taxi returned. Each Mayan tribe wore different colored embroidered clothing, short or long pants, and different colorful headwraps.

Walking through this small village of San Juan, a group of seven or eight curious little children began to collect in my wake. These kids were pointing at me chanting "Maximon! Maximon!" They were smiling and laughing. I had no idea what this meant, but I stopped and smiled back.

My Spanish skills were minimal, and feeling the need to make better contact, I reached into may knapsack for candies and small treats. The children happily snatched at these gifts while cheering. However, the third time I reached into my bag, I felt a weird sensation go through my hand and shivers travel up my forearm. Thinking nothing of this I again extending the treats I had garnered to the remaining outstretched hands. Suddenly their facial expressions changed and then they shrieked and bolted away in all directions. "Aiyee! Yoo!" They looked terrified and then I looked at my hand. Bright red blood was rushing from one finger and dripping profusely to the ground in a steady stream. A forgotten knife blade in my knapsack had done some damage on my index finger. Now the pain became more noticeable.

After the boat arrived, I learned that the kids following me thought I was a spiritual guide due to my skin color. *Maximon* is a god-like traditional superstition character. A figurative replica of this human formed entity is secretly moved from house to house. A priest guards this station and counsels those coming with special requests. The individual must bring food, money, liquor, or cigarettes as reparation. A few years later, I was able to find a willing guide to find where *Maximon* was in temporary residence. The figure of this entity was a life sized, colorfully dressed, male donning hat and smoking a cigar. Subsequent observance of a ceremony involving this mysterious character, produced photographs later published.

After building a house in San Marcos, another small lake village inhabited by another Mayan tribal group, I noticed a disturbing factor. This village which had been quiet, peopled by by raw primitive types. Naked women and children washed washed clothes and bathed themselves in the lake, things changed. Two churches were now in competition with the Catholics for parishioners. These new edifices had been built on opposite sides of small joining hills. The silence was disrupted twice daily by loudspeakers booming long sermons, prayers, and drab sounding gospel songs. Worse on Sundays their evangelical sounds clashed like wars in increased decibels. There was a sad addition, the Periodic blasting of fireworks and canons fired off on weekend celebrations. In just five years things in this part of the world had really changed. I would have to censor my own proclivity for being nude on my own property.

In a town called, **Esquipulas**, I found that a life-size sculpture of the black Jesus figure has attracted worshippers for over one hundred years. Free to roam and photograph indiscriminately, I observed scores of notes testifying to confirmed miracles resulting from contact with the black symbol of the Christ. The black Jesus is, accurate although opposite typical white images American and European media has traditionally propagated.

EGYPT. Stationed throughout the city, on virtually every street corner were young soldiers standing at rigid attention with bayoneted riles. Clearly, for me, there would be no jogging outdoors here in **Cairo**. An assassination had taken place at the hotel across the street from where our World Congress of Poets group resided. We were official government guests. There was still tension in the air. During one of several televised interviews, I casually placed my hand on the covered shoulder of the female TV interviewer. My intent was to ensure that we were close enough in the screen frame. She did not interpret my move had innocent intent. Looking sharply at me with a hard glare she said acidly,

"Sir! My husband is in the audience. You must not touch me!" I was shocked and somewhat embarrassed. However, I managed to keep the conversational dialogue flowing as if no rebuke had happened.

I felt happy to have seen top tourist sites, capturing photos and enjoying the restful cruise up and down the Nile. Initially, I had gotten mixed up with the wrong travelling group, and spent a few anxious hours with international geologists. Their ID tags read "RASM". This did not mean they were racism experts headed for a local forum. I had made a terrible assumption. These men were scientist reporting on shifting plates deep beneath the earth's surface. Obviously, I had suffered a brain cramp. Luckily, their conference host made sure that I arrived to the port, at what seemed like miles away, just in the nick of time to board for the Nile River cruise.

Performing with poet colleagues over a two-day period was exciting. For three days we packed houses and the audiences responded with enthusiasm. Thunderous applause for poetry? Here? Who would have thought? Some of us ranted about the war in Kuwait, political leadership, romance, and peace goals in general. We had the honor of meeting Madame Mubarak, the wife of the president. I even kissed the back of her hand. However, the aftermath for some of us foreigners trying to relax brought an unexpected anti-climax. Four of us, from the poets group convened together back in our designated hotel. We agreed to meet in the lobby cafe to unwind. We competed creating impromptu poetry lines showing our admiration of the local Egyptian tour guide, Amani Selah, who had caught our fancy. We all agreed she was exceptionally hot and sexy. Each one of us admitted having made attempts at scoring a date with her. I was happy to not being forced to masquerade wearing the mask of a saint.

As we relaxed over beverages a sudden commotion a few tables away disturbed the peaceful moment of levity we enjoyed. Three men, wearing headdress and national garb from an indistinguishable country, suddenly were struggling with hotel security. Shouting and yelling, chairs were knocked over and heavy metal object were heard hitting the floor. After the loud men had been ushered away we continued reliving our excitement about the poetry past program. Shortly, however, our hotel Concierge rushed to where we sat and urged us to immediately go to our rooms. "What was all the commotion about a few minutes ago?", someone asked. The hotel worker replied, "Oh, those men were outsiders and they wanted to talk to you all. But we had been watching them because of their suspicious behavior. Two of those men had knives, and one had a gun." We immediately hurried to our rooms. One female poet refused to go to her room alone. I am told most stayed awake all night worrying about which poet reading had been disturbing enough to incite a potential radical over-the-top reaction. Our wild guesses concluded that that group of party-crashers may have had bad intentions. Perhaps the TV interviewer's husband had succeeded in tracking me down.

ISRAEL. One weekend while in **Haifa**, a group of three men, identifying themselves as the parents of two students in my college classes back in Illinois. These visitors came to my hotel. They extended an invitation to be a guest at their home.

I accepted this invite and two or three hours later we arrived at their village. The name was about some kind of lion. This was somewhere in the Palestinian occupied region. They told me that this village was residence of around seven hundred families. Everyone was related to each other either way through marriage or birth. The father of one of my students back in America, was a large man with girth reminding me of, Pavrotti, the Italian singer. He was light skinned with short hair and dark, bushy mustache. He said that he owned an automotive dealership, and one day took me to Chinese restaurant he also claimed to own.

During mealtime in the evening, we sat around a spacious dining table, twelve men, all related to each other. The women did not eat until afterward. Then they ate in the kitchen while we men ate, drank wine, and sang and danced together. My host encouraged me to try dancing with a wine bottle perched atop my head to mimic his act of drunken skill.

Also, while in Jerusalem I felt comfortable and accepted being a dark skinned black among many whites. There was no suggestion of intolerant negativity. Our poets group also enjoyed a musical variety show put on by a local Jewish-Palestinian youth organization. We were amazed that a group inside the confines of Israel actively promoted cultural harmony. One photographic highlight were the pile of shoes shaped into a high wide mound. These had last been worn victims of the Holocaust. Also meeting several Jewish soldiers, young females shouldering AK-47 rifles, reminded me that these countrymen would never be defenseless victims again.

GERMANY. I had driven all around Germany taking photographs of historic churches, statues, and graffiti. I had been far north to **Emden** and crossed the border into **Strasbourg** from Switzerland. By my being married to Brigitte, we had been given the privilege to drive a relatives' automobile. This car sported a large, colorful team flag of Bayern's team that prominently hung from the rearview mirror. A relative was a member of the professional soccer team.

However, being a mixed couple in Germany, it was thought a good strategy to give other Germans a reason to think that I was one of the few black team members. At first, we had no hassles. One day while walking the streets in Munich, I was not so lucky.

A short white fellow quickly hopped form a distant ledge where he had been sitting with his buddies. He quickly crossed the broad square and approached me from behind. My wife and step-daughter quickened their steps and then alarmed me as they began to trot away. Then they sprinted. I looked out of the corner of my eye as the young guy came abreast and bumped me roughly with his shoulder. I stopped and looked him in the eyes. His mouth formed into a sneer as he said some German words. Running away was not in my mind. Why should I run?

Why did my wife and daughter run. Why they were afraid I did not know. But now it was clear the guy wanted to fight. I shouted at him. English.

"Hey! What's your problem?" After a moment of staring I turned a continued to walk. He snarled German words again. He pushed me. As I turned raising my fist shaking it at him. In the short distance behind us I could also see the gang of guys he had left intently watching us. The hateful stare down continued for a few more seconds. I then slowly turned and walked away. With each step I anticipated a kick, I had made up my mind if this happened a fight would be on. I would strike back. I had done my beset to avoid the physical conflict that seemed eminent. I did not look back. That next push or blow never came. The guy was smaller, and I clearly outweighed him. It all seemed foolish to me as I could easily predict the outcome of the first wave. However, I knew that his gang also had made a chess move. The little guy had been a pawn. I guess we both were lucky. I thought my image of being a positive cultural representative had almost gone up in smoke. At that moment and time there was no way for me to escape being labeled "enemy". My mere presence had made me a target. Fortunately, having been conditioned in my youth to have discipline allowed me to steel my emotions. This was not the first time a potential volatile situation had been averted.

Visiting the famed **Dachau** concentration camp, I also had a chilling observation. Obvious to me was the fact that Hitlers message of Nazism has not died out with the defeat of the Third Reich. Young, pale faced, Storm Troopers, marched through the solemn memorial of the extermination site. They yelled racial epithets and chants, as their boots rhythmically stomped eerie echoes on the drab concrete floors. It was clear to me that years conditioning negative of constant had not been erased. Sadly, these were young people, and their parents may have passed on their ignorant racial negativities. Old habits die hard.

During this European trip my Hayfever became particularly troublesome. Locating a recommended acupuncture practitioner, I found his allergy treatment effective and service amenable. However, on one occasion after treatment, I left that office with two, thin steel needles still stuck in my head unnoticed. This was a comical sight when discovered. I chose to believe this oversight by the specialist an accident.

Some years later, during another visit to Germany, this time I was leaving Berlin after my solo photography exhibition. Meeting an African girl, I engaged in conversation that led me driving her to a club where she worked. I had seen scores of mixed couples, even some with children in tow, during the recent street *Karnivale* held days earlier. However, seeing this girl was one of the few times I had seen a fellow dark countryman in this area of town. We managed to hook up and I became convinced that my old game was back in the groove. It felt great to not posturize, pretending to be an innocent lamb, not a wolf.

INDIA. Highlighting this trip was the excellent tour, my host, Arun Gandhi turned out to be, also the variety of Graffiti shots captured via camera. The monetary crisis did not directly affect me until after my arrival in **Mumbai**. ATM machines were empty and the new currency had not yet been distributed. I had to watch a few machines and depend on cues from the hotel staff for timing arrival of currency in order to beat foot traffic for obtaining money. It was fascinating to visit Gandhi's Grandfather's house. Getting into this country proved easy with only a few hiccups, but getting out was a nightmare. The initial entry was costly, the exit was costlier.

Gandhi had a driver take us around to explore various parts of the city. Touring the home of his legendary grandfather, Mahatma Gandhi, and hearing stories about Martin Luther King's visit to the same place were inspiring. I was told Dr. King slept overnight in this museum place in the same bedroom where Gandhi had been born. Arun's family prepared a fine meal as I enjoyed more conversation in the privacy of their home. Great public respect was obvious at many places we ventured in this city whether beaches or business enterprises. It was refreshing to see most public advertisements and billboards not populated by white faces. Brown and dark skin as symbols of beauty made me feel welcome and accepted. I blended in among students at one university, chatted with students, and photographed a team practicing Cricket. This sports game I had never seen before in real life. This was the same feeling of positive identification felt when I had visited other third-world countries like Egypt, South Africa, and the Caribbean islands.

ZIMBABWE. The sweet smells of earth greeted me each morning. This was different than the usual smog, or dust bowls that blinded. Safely arriving in the southern region of the African continent had not been without unexpected drama. The airline baggage handlers had gone on strike when our plane had stopped in **Lisbon**, Portugal. This meant an unplanned pause staying overnight in Lisbon. I was happy because this allowed me to venture leisurely exploring the city with camera in hand. Now, I was stoked finally in **Harare**. I would get to float on Zambia River, eat tasty crocodile meals, drink Stella beers, walk through the grand botanical gardens, and ultimately see the grand Victoria Falls.

Attending a leadership workshop at the University of Zimbabwe allowed an opportunity to meet Ministers Robert Mugabe, and H.M. Murerna, Minister of Culture. Our group enjoyed lunch prepared by locals. It was at this time I decided to take the advice Senator Paul Simon had given me during our interview session back in Washington, D.C.. Simon from Illinois, and also author of the book, The Tongue-Tied American, said, "Young man, if you do have an opportunity to visit South Africa, do it!" And now, thanks to his encouragement here I was, months later, close to that country's border.

I proceeded to purchase a flight to Johannesburg, only to receive disappointing news. My passport had expired one day earlier. Now I was unable to go anywhere. I was stuck. This emergency luckily was settled in two days, and while collecting my new passport an agent advised me to stop in and see Ms. Bridgewater at the American Consulate office. Be sure to let them know that you, as an American citizen are there. I looked forward to having at least another prospective contact in that foreign country. I wondered if in "Jo'burg" I would feel at home, as I did in Zimbabwe. Time would tell.

SOUTH AFRICA. I could hardly believe what I was hearing. This interrogation could only mean that I was under suspicion, perhaps a Spy. Why, or by whom was not clear. However, the person quizzing me would not let up. She was a middle age, hard-looking black African woman. I had noticed her standing off to the side in the large office when I was meeting the Consulate in **Durban**. Afterward, she had offered to drive me back to my hotel. Her short wiry, black hair had grey patches at the temples. Stern chocolate skin taunt around a serious looking mouth seemed to prevent smiles. That she was dead serious was no doubt. Deep lines that crept away from her eyes, suggested many years attending to matters of gravity. Apparently, my presence in her country was a matter of concern. She seemed wound tight and tense. Her words drove this point home.

"Tell me again. What are you doing here? What do you want?" A long pause filled the close quarters of the parked car.

"I already told you. I am a professor in Illinois on vacation. I am trying to finish working on my manuscript about my years of human relations work in America. I have never been to South Africa and now have an opportunity to do so. What more do you need?" My voice level was screechy and high with exasperation. I could not conceal my impatience and irritation. I planned on ordering a suit tailored for the occasion. Customs suits were cheap in Africa, my discovery from hours of window shopping and snapping my camera. But now we were parked on a dirt road outside the city. The route my volunteer driver had taken seemed precariously in the wrong direction. My interrogator's strong looking veined hands with tough, lean fingers tightened on the steering wheel. I began to imagine those same journeyman fingers griping my neck taking my breath away in a deadly fashion. Suddenly I was scared for some unknown reason. Her words had a deadly ring.

"Well, this all sounds suspicious to me. I need to know more. Why do you want to come to the Fireside meeting? Issues in Africa do not concern you. Nothing is relevant to your American work. You say you are a teacher. Why you here? Who are you really?"

"Okay. Okay. Look, I do know something about affirmative action and our local government activities. I want to meet Professor Tanaka and hear his views. He is a prominent scholar in the U.S.. I may have something to add from a practitioner's perspective. I am also am a poet and Professor Kunene offered to give me a ride since he is also going there. I did not ask to attend the Fireside meeting, I had not known about it until Consular Bridgewater invited me. Since I know that you work for her, you should know more about what is going on than I. All I know is the meeting time. I do not have the address." I assumed that I could be flexible in that setting.

However, the African woman looked at me in silence for several seconds. Her sharp black eyes tried to bore a hole through my head. Finally, she started the car again, and shifting from each gear in a ferocious manner, we made a U-turn. Gunning the motor we were in front of my hotel in a matter of minutes. No more words were spoken until the car stopped.

"Here we are. Enjoy your visit. Be careful."

That was it. Her words seemed insincere and mechanical. I closed the car door respectfully and waited for the car to disappear before hurrying to the clothing shop. I would soon pick up a fine looking gray striped business suit. Traveling light I had not brought anything formal to wear. I was happy the suit did not cost over $200 USD, but it looked a like in the $900-1000 range.

What a bargain. I now splurged on a pair of black hard soled shoes. My tennis footwear did not go along with the new outfit: white collar, short-sleeve shirt, and necktie. I was ready to make an appearance.

While in South Africa, I did the recommended tours: Table-Top Mountain, Seweto, taking snapshots, chatting with friendly whites and browns (folk of India extraction called "coloreds") enjoying the pristine beaches. The streets of Johannesburg teemed with pedestrians, there was tension in the air. It had been also my pleasure to attend a few entertainment shows, rubber boot dancing troupes. Another surprise was a Motown musical tribute to Diana Ross and the Supremes. The show was fantastic as the song and costumes on point. and I met the local performers after the show and invited them for drinks and snacks. Five showed up in the hotel lobby nervously looking over their shoulders. They informed me they were forbidden to go to certain places to eat or drink. It was late at night after their performance. There still were restrictions to their movements although they worked within the city limits. Our interaction was strained, they looked at me as if I was from another planet.

While staying at the Holiday Inn in Jo'burg, I wandered into the hotel gift shop. There I met the owner who had fascinating Shona sculptures displayed. She was a middle aged black African woman and seemed quite knowledgeable about the sculptured stonework. Soon I learned that her husband, Roy Clark was an art curator, a white man. They would be the only racially mixed couple that I knew in South Africa. After sharing lunch, I was later offered the chance to visit the famous sculpture gardens. While there I noticed a few American tourists gravitated to an authentic spiritual man, who was labeled a "Witch Doctor". After this walnut colored man, adorned in robe and feathered headdress, granted me permission to capture his image, I wandered thru the hot, dusty stone field. There I met a black American female sculpting hard at work chopping and carving. Amana Johnson, from Oakland, California, had won an international travel grant to continue her craft as an artist. About a year later, I had the opportunity to assist both, Johnson and Clark to make presentations at my college in the US.

On my final day in Africa I barely reached the airport on time. I was relieved to leave, but still miffed at not hearing from poet Kunene, nor attending the Bridgewater Fireside meeting.

Apparently, I had been vetted by security and failed for reasons unknown. I departed with a manuscript unfinished, but with a souvenir of a smashing looking fashion outfit. I suppose my timing for this visit was severely off. The meeting was scheduled to be at Bridgewater's home. She had been easy to talk to and was quite attractive, but I never found out more. Maybe I had been in deep water with no clue. When I departed, however, somewhere among my camera rolls, was the stunning image of a mulatto colored girl whom I had caught in the hotel lobby.

Her taxi spirited her away too quickly. I had never seen such a beautiful angelic face in all my travels. But this would not be the last country in which my presence was viewed as an American government Spy. I became a different target, man with a new burden to bear.

FRANCE. While driving from south of France to **Paris**, in the north, I found myself unable to find my hotel. This was more than confusing because I had the specific address. Using my all but forgotten French words I could recall, I received specific verbal directions from a police officer. He had also pointed the hotel out in the distance, but it was located on another street. Yet, after this I was still driving around in circles. The one-way streets converged unpredictably with two-way traffic patterns. It took at least forty minutes for me to resolve this confused situation. When I finally saw the hotel again, I decided to simply park my rented vehicle and walk to check in. Years earlier someone had remarked, whomever had designed the streets of Paris, must have been drunkards or madmen. I could attest to those streets being randomly designed like a jigsaw puzzle.

Aside from the heavenly cuisine I sampled around and about in this country, I discovered that french people generally had haughty attitudes toward foreigners who did not address them using French lingo. Through experimentation I discovered many would pretend to no understand English, However, no matter how poorly my deteriorated language skills had become. By simply trying to use my vocabulary, this frequently earned their respect. After demonstrating these efforts, only then would people use English that made interactions pleasant and less strenuous. Language is a key factor in creating communication common ground. I Iearned the importance of being sensitive to image impressions when and where this mattered.

GREECE. Standing in the Athens airport I was amazed while listening to the exchange in front of me. A white woman, obviously a foreign was engaged in heated dialogue with much vitriol. The woman behind the ticket counter was not backing down.

"Just who do you think you are? You're raising your voice making demands. We can only do so much. I can't make planes come and go whenever I choose. Do I look like the pilot? You need to take a break and back off!" But the angry traveler then chose to rachet the emotional climate.

"Well, I don't care what excuse there is, you bitch. I paid to get there at 5:00 pm and I arrived at 10:00 pm. I'm tired of such sloppy fucking service in this place! I can't stand you people!" As she huffed away. The ticket lady shouted at the retreating back.

"That's okay! WE don't like you Americans either!"

Being next, I stopped closer to the counter attempting to defuse the tension said in a comical voice.

"What about me? I'm American. Do I count?" I put on a sheepish expression and tried a childish, high pitched voice. She looked at me laughing.

"Oh, you're okay… it's the rest of them we can't stand!"

However, the Greek lady words were not entirely accurate. In this part of the world I could not wear special hat to disguise my cultural identity. Although I had at one point enjoyed the private hospitality by a local family I had known before my trip to Greece, a mix of experiences convinced me to remain objective. Regarding racial or cultural prejudice, there were plenty of examples on both sides of the spectrum. An example was my taxi driver had stopped fifty yards away from my hotel entrance. He took my luggage out of the car and simply pointed saying, "Your taxi is over there." No traffic blocked the street. I could see other taxis drive to the entrance and deposit their fare. My driver simply did not drive me to the entrance. An hour later, I found myself in a terrible room, although the prices were quite high. Chatting with another white American, I discovered this person was also experiencing similar unpleasantness. In Athens I inwardly failed to measure up to the confident image I had fantasized being exhibited. When visiting the historic Olympic stadium where races had been held a few thousand years ago I was humbled. Being a former competitive track runner myself, I had vowed upon arriving at this site I would take a casual lap jogging around the four-hundred meter oval. Once inside this location, however, a plethora of excuses prevented me for executing my goal. Either pride or fear overcame me as my legs became stone blocks. I could only sit inside the stadium watching other brave souls sprint and jog around the historic oval.

Flying to the island of Crete I found the hospitality civil, food and service excellent. This was my experience with private entrepreneurs. Santorini was equally impressive and photography win- win no matter what or where I chose to focus my camera. Perhaps, when on the nudist island where I chose "Super Paradise" over "Little Paradise" someone may have played a prank on me. After situating myself sharing an umbrella with a tourist couple, I finally decided to take a nude dip into the heavenly clear, blue water. After soaking several minutes returning to my shade patch became impossible. The white towel marker I had left hanging on the umbrella wooden spokes had disappeared. AS far as I could tell, I was the only black, non-suntanned person at this beach.

The sun and sand were extremely hot. Tortuous. Several minutes I walked the entire area searching among the vast number of lobster red, and brown oiled nude bodies. People simply looked away chuckling. Eventually. Returning the backside of the sandy beach where chairs and umbrella rental stands were located, a loud welcoming voice boomed at me.

"Oh there you are Professor Arron! You look lost! Are you okay?"

I was surprised these beach workers knew my name and occupation. I had not told them. However, at that moment my priority was to locate my towel, shade, and personal belongings. I had not taken these items into the water.

"I'm okay", I lied with bravado. "I'm just looking for my clothes."

"Oh. Okay. If you need any help let us know", one workers said chuckling, "You'll probably find them where you left them last. You probably should just get back in the water and cool off some more."

Taking that advice, I trekked back to the beginning and resumed my soaking. The hot sun was unrelenting. Thankfully, the cool waters had a calming effect. At this point four hot G-Strip wearing nymphs appeared out of nowhere posing at my potential exit point. They stood near waiting. I continued soaking much longer than planned. Remaining submerged, I became colder, my genitals seemed to shrivel into raisin size. Eventually, the girls departed, I quickly found my belongings. I was quite relieved, perhaps more that I had escaped intense body scrutiny from a group of sexy chicks wearing G-Strings, than finding my bag of goods.

However, a news story still lurked in back of my mind. On one small Greek island, a black man had been involved in a fight between his group of tourists and Greek locals. Separated from his group he was murdered. No perpetrators had been charged.

RUSSIA. After surviving a long grueling Trans-Siberian train ride from Inner Mongolia to **Irkutsk**, and **Ekaterinburg**. After four days we reached **Moscow** which was an impressive city. Onion shaped rooftops simply pricked my imagination and expectations. My eyes were constantly widened in surprise by sights, opulent palaces, sculptures that glittered in gold, and the latest technological conveniences. Each city visited seemed to be a jewel of parks, historic palaces, and fountains. This was not the Russia I expected. Even the people were friendly and welcoming, and some went beyond the call of duty being helpful. On at least three occasions my guides volunteered to take me to the address I sought. Their sincere insistence overrode my objections. Like the Chinese they would say, "It's my duty." My hosts families at two

Bed and Breakfast establishments were genuinely entertaining. I had to admit that most, if not all folk I met, were a hardy, hardworking lot. No one seemed soft, or weak. I doubt that I could survive harsh winters with temperatures minus sixty degrees and lower. Here, however, the least of my worries was about trying to fit in.

Food dishes were indescribable, from caviar laden creations, to wonderful meats wrapped in grape leaves. Fresh fish dishes caught from Lake Baikal were out of this world. However, in **St. Petersburg**, I found that everyman's wants, needs, and desires easily satisfied. By the time I had reached this city, obtaining good reading materials written by my favorite Russian authors, I was more than ready to relax more than just my worn-out feet. Russian writers Chekov and Pushkin would have understood.

In St. Petersburg, on a main street a short distance from the upscale Sex Museum, one narrow doorway advertised a massage salon upstairs. This was my second visit to Russia, and also this city so I felt quite at ease moving around. Venturing the steep passage, I ambled past a large man, seated at the halfway point. His uniform suggested he was the security guard. Inside the salon was a glossy notebook, the menu for the type girl to select for personal bodywork.

Disappointed at not finding dark-skinned girls among the offerings, an attractive Korean girl was my choice.

When the girl I selected appeared in my lavishly decorated room, her picture book appearance had not done her justice. The person who appeared before me was like a perfect human robot. From stem to stern it was as if I beheld an automated fantasy who could whisper and speak.

She oiled my body and massage every inch of my person. At several massage stages I attempted to interrupt her work. It would have been obvious even to a blind person that my erection was strained rock-hard needing relief. But, still she continued working methodically like a robot, at several point pinning my wrists, whispering not yet. Even after shedding her scant lingerie, the oil on my body soon glistened on her firm, silky smooth, curvaceous torso. She slowly moved her body gliding over mine, gently massaging in sensuous circles. This massage professional had perfectly shaped long limbs, an abdomen the looked man-made, and full breasts that impossibly did not sag. Even her nipples felt hard and dangerous. Finally, unable to stand this teasing, I thrust her off in an attempt to take control. She immediately sprang off the bed, headed for the shower looking back at me with a smile. I was not an angel. I knew what this was about.

CHINA. In China, I felt much psychological relief not being faced with Christian churches and bothersome evangelicals. Seeing smiling and sleeping Buddhas made me feel comfortable. I relaxed more into pursuing my artistic goals. In order to survive on the mainland I found it easier to try fitting in versus fighting against the massive currents of cultural differences. Each adventure reinforced it was far better to be flexible than to expect things in China to be done like back home in America. I learned to quietly accept red envelopes stuffed with money, traditionally given as gifts to show appreciation. Westerners might call these bribes. On special celebrations family members also expected to receive red envelopes. However, when I showed up to photograph public show, in this instance a local Chinese Opera House, I was surprised when casually presented a red envelope with several one hundred yuan inside. On another occasion after a televised singing performance, I was surprised to receive a red envelope that contained one thousand yuan. The expression, "Black Whistles" is another new thing that I was ignorant of until attending a few professional sports events. At CBA (basketball) events fans would complain about referees ignoring infractions among players. At soccer matches fans would throw debris onto the playing fields and yelling, "Black Whistles! Black Whistles! Black whistles again!" It seemed that Chinese fans expected games to be thrown or one sided, obviously controlled by referees and judges.

Money talks. This seemed to be reality not only in Beijing, but everywhere else in China where high rollers clearly are in control. One incident publicized in the news was about a young fellow who, while driving fatally killed a pedestrian. He seemed blasé about the accident, saying "I'm not worried about this matter. My father is rich. He will take care of this." In school classrooms, students also talked about middle school experiences where parents routinely give gifts to teachers or administrators to ensure they kids will be given special attention. Parents who fail to intercede with special favors is the difference between whether a student is seated in front of the classroom or in the rear. Also, parents, and or school administrators can assure a failing student passes or graduates, if special favors are given. Bribery is a norm in China. I personally had to deal with this factor in several academic institutions.

Chinese cuisine was one of my favorite experiences along with spas. I found donkey meat sandwiches, served between taco like bread, quite delicious with hot spices. Boiled snake soup and a variety of sea foods were addictive along with barbequed vegetables, like spicy green onions and mushroom, served on skewers. Chinese versions of pastas or noodles stuffed with meat or vegetables were also tasty delights.

Footbaths and spas are as popular in China as gasoline stations and Seven Elevens are everywhere in the world. While spas do not have, global brands, whole body care is a necessity in the Orient where hard work is expected of everyone. Laziness is frowned upon, and hard workers are pampered. A footbath can often involve a short full-body massage. Spa salons usually involved hot soaking pools in rooms with theatre size television screens. Private baths also existed in higher tiered establishments. Ears are routinely deep cleaned for wax removal.

Health food: carrots, cherry tomatoes, apples, bananas and tea with salty snacks may be served on gratis. There was no time limit on how long you remained in certain spas. Whether high-end luxurious, or low-end spartan, in most spa facilities my skin color did not matter.

However, at one facility in **Changsha** city, four girls were paraded into my room to be selected as my private Masseuse. Receiving treatment in a large public room, as opposed to private, is often one's choice. The first girl I finally chose initially ran from shrieking shouting unintelligible words as she departed. This occurred only a few seconds we had been left alone. I could hear the male host outside the room attempting to persuade her to return. The next girl entering was happily smiling and willing to massage me pleasantly with no hassle. I tipped her generously, recalling being massaged another time by two workers simultaneously. These girls had pulled and pinched my skin and muscles most unpleasantly. Finally, I had to repeatedly yell commands ordering them to stop. I learned early that people could easily communicate their feelings despite language barriers.

There was one unforgettable sexual experience that occurred in the city of **Jilin**. Telling the taxi driver that I wanted to go to the best spa salon in the city, we soon stopped at a huge gothic structure with large gold lions squatting beside the wide glass door entrance. Inside were lavish decorations, soft, thick carpeting and faint sounds of strings playing traditional oriental music. At first, I attempted using my limited broken Chinese words to convey my request. Quickly when we were alone and private my masseuse shushed me to be silent as she put her forefinger against her smiling slips and then mine. Next kisses followed tracing a slow pattern from my belly button and further below. All that I remember of this event was a whirlwind of action. At one point I thought my gonads would disappear down an over-achieving, greedy throat. This had been a first and there were moments I thought I would not survive. My lost moment of clarity returned after I had showered.

In China, several of my cameras were used until they became burnt out and needed repair or were replaced. I was struck by the colorful variety of wall murals and graffiti art reflected government themes, as well as, radical individual expressions. When I had first entered the mainland, morning work crews were washing away or painting over graffiti. Years later, many areas were designated specifically for personalized individual radical or fantasy character themes. University and Middle School art students tended to contribute to much of this visual art. Shopping mall walkways displayed either Che Guevara or other revolutionary figures creatively. There were so many architectural surprises that combined modernity with ancient styles, that my jaws repeatedly dropped with awe. Capturing unique photography was almost impossible to avoid.

"Put your camera away! Do it quickly!" these words were from a friend as we walked a city street in Hunan province. A group of police and young men wearing red arm bands, were viciously beating a middle-aged woman. She was lying on the ground clutching her throat. I felt the urge to intervene as my friend pulled me away and said, "Just keep walking. You don't want to get involved. This matter does not concern you. You are not Chinese! You are a foreigner!"

As we walked away, I kept my camera hidden. The men continued to laugh while beating the woman. I do know of cases where black foreigners have been arrested for merely defending themselves when attacked by Chinese. Victims or anyone defined as an offender by Chinese authority risk being jailed or deported. While I was happy about many publication opportunities that came my way, but there were a few raw business deals.

TIBET. Catching my breathe was suddenly a problem that had ensued with a lingering headache and a spat of nausea. I had been warned about the rare air when being high in the forbidden mountains. But I imagined myself able to handle this unique situation. This proved me a bit foolhardy, as I lay in bed for one day, and walked slowly when I dared to venture out and see shows and special prearranged traditional dance and singing performances. As for cuisine, the roast lamb, Yak milk, Yak butter and bread were unusually tasty. I must admit, however, having been totally mystified in awe of pilgrims travelling prone on stomachs and knees in a large plaza. This worship ritual continued for hours in the heat of day until sunset.

While this environment seemed serenely otherworldly, there was one dramatic cultural glitz. Apparently, being accompanied by, Rainbow, an attractive Chinese companion. Serving as my guide and translator, Rainbow was alert and sensitive regarding the obviously unequal service displayed toward us. Several patrons arriving after we had been seated waiting to place our food order, received their food long before ours. Rainbow, my companion and long-haired dictionary, became increasingly upset. Her silence and intense expression caused me to ask: "Hey… what's eating you? Is everything okay?"

"No!" Her response angry and loud, was totally out of character. I had known her for several months to be mild mannered and pleasant. Her occupation was a desk manager of a high-end international hotel in Beijing. She paused and then continued. "I don't like it here. They are just being nasty towards us. Earlier I had asked our Waiter why our food had taken such a long time to arrive. Our order had been simple. He said, that me and my nigger could wait. I hate this place!" Suddenly without warning she stood and threw her plastic chopsticks against the surface of the table. Next, she angrily snatched one edge of the white tablecloth off the table. The loud crash of tableware startled the noisy diners for a few seconds. "Let's go!" Rainbow said and strode stone-faced toward the entrance and out the door. I followed keeping my eyes straight fastened on her retreating back. I readied myself expecting a staff worker to bolt out of the restaurant to charge after us. No one followed. This was a bazaar scene in total contrast to the serenity of a place so close to heaven.

During the remainder of that trip Rainbow sulked more and became less talkative. Eventually, I found myself in the small hotel spa seeking a full-body massage. The sturdy plain looking woman was skillful. Her hands had soothed my aching back and legs, plying hand and finger movements for several minutes. Slowly she had assisted me to turn over on my back. She gently caressed my pubic hairs and erect penis. Suddenly without warning or invitation she had ripped off her own clothes and sat astride my naked body in a matter of seconds. The regular expected massage had ended, but still we were on the clock. Outside, nearby, holy pilgrims wandered and twirled their handheld ornate miniature prayer wheels. Already dazzled by the sights inside the holy *Patola* edifice, and impossibly beautiful nature scenes, I tried my best to relax breathing the rarified air. Later I would spin a few large, metal plated Prayer Wheels, and walk solemn minded among the other mix of native and foreign worshippers. For me this did not feel hypercritical, because I believed as I do now, that God was and is big enough to accept me as I am.

CHAPTER 26

New Pathways

I am determined to slowly transition back into the "American Experience." Even in the ranks of informal teacher/public lecturer, the responsibility to inform remains. Now my eyes are wide open despite the weary three-day cross-country train ride to California from Silver Springs, Maryland. I feel like an alien in my own homeland. It's difficult to ignore the long caravans of homeless people wandering and shuffling about. Many wear unwashed military fatigues and push all their worldly belongings around in stolen metal shopping carts. I often see sunburned red-necks and dusty brown and black panhandlers working corners at busy traffic intersections. Overweight pedestrians of mixed ethnicities waddle on and off public buses. A few instigate unprovoked altercations with other passengers. Some folk spout loud monologues addressing the general public. A few others conduct long diatribes with imaginary partners. These sights are alarming and irritating to me. Back home in Las Vegas, while chatting with the black lady cutting my hair, she suddenly exclaimed indignantly, "I don't need no gun! I ain't gonna kill nobody!"

The defiance in her voice spoke volumes. Scenes of conscientious objectors in old war movies played in my mind: guys stubbornly refusing to pick up arms, even in the military, have been conditioned against any notion of physical self-defense. They believe that to kill is wrong, no matter the circumstance. Let others protect you or die believing that death is God's will.

They cry, don't be an agitator! Troublemakers deserve what they get. Such thinking befuddled me. I have been feeling free and flying. I had wanted to fly higher.

On one televised series I'm watching, *The Alaskans: Life Below Zero*, a homesteader teaches her children how to kill chickens for their dinner. Funneling the bird upside down into a metal tube that narrows to be only wide enough for the bird's head to protrude, death comes silently. The chicken's head is quickly lopped off without flying feathers and wild squawking.

The mother then tells her watchful children, who are between the ages of five and seven, "This is the humane way to kill your food. The chicken will not needlessly suffer."

In Hunan, I had watched a Chinese chef hypnotize a plump chicken by simply using one forefinger. After the bird was in a trance, the chef used a sharp knife to deftly slit the bird's throat. The feathered creature slowly became lifeless as a thin wire of blood trickled out and puddled on the earth. This chicken gradually weakened, and death came without alarm or surprise. Many would argue that this is a more humane way to present death to any living being. Yet images of that chicken's futile run toward an impossible exit remain etched in my memory. To me, it mirrors the plight of minority groups in America. We are turned out and upside down, some strung out more than others. It is a slow death.

Desperation, survival, and death have a great deal of relevance in our society today.

Achieving cultural harmony seems like a lost cause, an impossible dream of the past. My work as an educator in classrooms at home and abroad now force me to focus on realities of personal survival. In the U.S., it is impossible to dismiss the issue of personal security. In fact, as I write this, I have spent the past few days shopping to better arm myself. I'm not sure whether my ultimate weapon will be a larger deadly blade or a sexy, state-of-the-art firearm. I am tempted to become a gun owner. It is really scary here and increasingly impossible to ignore the ads for local firearms conventions. I am older, and clearly this is a country for the young, the wild, and foolish.

For those of us conditioned to a life on the fringes of American society, we must realize that success cannot be measured in terms of becoming socially accepted and treated fairly by all. Respect and social equality will never be simply *given* to all by all. These are things that must be demanded. This is the nature of life. We are all, like it or not, part of the Animal Kingdom. Kill or be killed is the cardinal rule of the jungle. Survival, by any means necessary, ultimately is what really matters. Fighting long enough to live another day is essential. For this to happen, we must first cultivate our abilities and skill sets and believe in ourselves. This is the magic we need.

In the final analysis, the civilized person knows that preparation is the key to survival. This is fundamental and our individual responsibility. It doesn't matter whether or not I am loved by every man and woman I meet. I fully believe in one truth: the ancient philosopher, Cicero, said, "In times of war, the law falls silent."

CHAPTER 27

Anxious Endings

I **did not want to be a laughingstock in the group**. Nor did I want to have an accident in my pants. My fourth marriage of twelve years had reached the inevitable end. The last day in that week everyone in the impromptu group would notice any unusual smell. For a few hours we had been in cramped quarters. After lectures and videos we waited for our turn in the plane, I heard a fear story. The tale made me think of a few of the negative consequences of skydiving. Three things to be avoided are vomiting, shitting one's pants, or "walking toward the light."

Today, I was a 'virgin' jumper. This would be my first time parachuting from a plane.

Hopefully, there would be many tomorrows. I would soon know what kind of 'stuff' I was made of. Was I crazy enough to jump. Perhaps I had harbored a death wish. Here I was venturing into disturbing behaviors again.

No one in my immediate family claimed to be mentally wrapped up tight, as plenty of spurious family lore lurked in the background. My mother's brother, Uncle Gene, avoided military service by 'playing crazy.' Subsequently, he spent several years in California's Cabrillo Beach Hospital for mental instability. When he was finally released into my grandmother's custody, his older sister—our mother—was reluctant to let us kids spend any time alone with him. We were told to never go into his room. That room was his 'jail cell.' In that room Uncle Gene holed-up for hours playing strange piano music on a rosewood upright. I heard his feet keeping time, thumping a rhythm on the wooden floor. He frequently laughed although alone in his room. He made that same "he, he, he" laugh when grandma took plates of food to his room during holiday dinners. Uncle Gene laughed a lot for no apparent reason. We were warned to never be alone with him. He was disturbed.

"Your uncle is not right in the head," dad said. "He plays jazz on that piano."

Not that dad modeled mental stability. Dad would have never admitted to having any 'demons,' but he certainly had them. He just dealt with them differently than Uncle Gene did.

Dad never laughed much. He was always serious and always 'right' about everything. I suppose his being a "Holy Roller" in his youth, a musician, and a storyteller shaped this particular trait. In church he would play the trumpet, piano, or guitar. The white-garbed, heavily perfumed old women got excited and flailed their arms wildly, jerked their bodies, or ran with abandon up and down the church aisles. His music was infectious, and he was convinced that the voice of God spoke directly to him. No one dared defy or refute his reality.

My younger brothers, five or six years old, had learned to follow his orders. They had been conditioned, just like I had, by countless whippings. Dad communicated commands to us fiercely in both voice and demeanor. Jump! Do not ask questions. Just do it!

"Get down, mister!" dad yelled as he drove his new green pickup truck in the alley behind our house. "Don't make me have to tell you again! Get down!"

My little brother, Buddy, had already been standing, struggling to balance himself on the moving truck bed. The next few seconds seemed like a strange nightmare. I remember my dad shouting and pointing, and then I saw my brother Buddy jumping. The fierce look on dad's face changed to a blank passive glare. He gripped the steering wheel, as the truck sped forward. My kid brother hit the pavement. Obviously little Buddy had misread dad's nonverbal cues. He could not have heard dad's words from inside the cab.

I had been standing at the back gate as dad had proudly driven his new truck out of the garage. The next thing I knew, my little brother was standing in the truck, dad was looked back and yelled. Buddy was jumping, and brakes screeched. The truck tires slid a few seconds and finally stopped. I ran to the scene. Buddy was violently shaking in the middle of the alley. His eyes were fixated on the truck and the man who had always taught us to jump when he said "Jump." Do not ask how high. Just do it. The monster was now running toward him. Little Buddy was shaking and sobbing, "Did I do okay, Daddy? Did I do okay?"

A few years later, this same little brother set fire to a field by our house. Little Buddy had become infatuated with the magic of matches and their little sparks. Perhaps this was a show of bridled anger. But independent action was power to bring change. He was not much different with his bridled anger than I had been at his age. Fifty years later, this same sibling became further brainwashed to an unbelievable degree. He had formed regular demonstration groups outside local churches. Entering White churches to disrupt worship services, was accompanied by his ranting tirades. Shouting phrases like, "You are false prophets! You preach lies and serve the devil!" These actions did not endear community residents or church goers to him or Bethel church in the desert. Eventually banned entry into one competing religious denomination, my sibling was arrested and fined. He had disturbed the peace. Buddy, the main instigator was indignant, telling everyone, "I don't mind suffering for Jesus. This is what all believers should do. Being a warrior for Christ is what the bible teaches." His final act was his arrest and confinement. He had led a group of church picketers holding printed placards reading, "Devil Worshipers Enter Here!"

This episode furthered solidified our family fringe cult brand. It is difficult to disassociate our past family brainwashing from anti-social behaviors. Even one of my older sisters, Lollie, set a dangerous precedent using the fire approach. She is reputed to have tried burn down a campus building at Columbia University in New York. Rumor had it that she had deliberately set that campus fire, after hearing voices. Apparently, investigations discovered obstacles to her being granted a master's degree was a contributing factor. To go over the edge, or behave with schizophrenic tendencies is all in the family. And I thought that skydiving was a not radical behavior. I wanted to really fly. Some close to me viewed this disturbing behavior. What was I trying to do, kill myself, they asked.

Before boarding the plane for my first official recorded jump, there was a lot of waiting around. It was early, and I was starving. My six o'clock a.m. wake-up call, and cold forty-minute motorcycle trek to the Chicago Sky Dive School, had left no time for breakfast. My body yearned for a hot cup of coffee. I certainly could have used something. Anything. Thank god there was Coke and vending machines with packaged chips and cookies.

Before I knew it, I was in my jumpsuit, harnessed and crammed into the brand-new 'Super Outer' airplane with fifteen other jumpers, including two other 'newbies' with their jump partners. *What would happen after I left the safety of the airplane.* This thought worried me.

Would I remember the few basics I had been taught. Would I freeze and become mentally paralyzed? I wouldn't know until I actually jumped. Suddenly, I had the tremendous need to expel what I hoped was only gas. I farted loudly.

At 13,500 feet, a warning buzzer went off. The ground now resembled a collection of old, faded, antique quilts. The first group of experienced pros jumped first. My cameraman went next. And then it was out turn. There was counting, but no one said the word "Jump!" All I could think about was how hungry I was and how I needed to arch my body and remember to look at my altimeter and pull the rip-cord and breathe and tuck my legs properly with my partner's and not look at the ground so I wouldn't throw up and not to grab the bar over the plane's open doorway and not to open my mouth and remember the cameraman wants… what?

And suddenly I'm falling... I hear nothing but a mighty rushing wind... is this the Holy Ghost?... I'm freefalling on my back for days... there's the plane, and then it's gone... now I'm floating on my stomach... we're floating... we're falling... this is fun! We spin slowly, and my partner seems to be kicking at the air. My ears are clogged, and it's hard to hear. My nose is being stretched open wide with too much air. I seem to be breathing water. My eye goggles seem to be slipping. And here comes the camera guy again, floating close and then away from my face. We spin in a slow, lazy circle. I hear nothing but a roar.

Joe, my jump instructor, pulled my left wrist in front of my face. I looked at the altimeter and realized it was going past the number five. I heard his voice say "Pull!" My hand had already been on the ripcord handle this whole time, and I had forgotten about it. His hand closed over mine as I pulled. I swallowed, and suddenly in my mind I heard an old poem:

DIVING HIGH

I swim in a restless ocean of air

Forever on a clear blue visible glare.

This I want to enjoy for eternity's chair

Remembering the super rush of free-fall

Wanting to scream and yell wanting to stall

Become an Airhead through it all.

"Where is Chicago?" I asked.

My jump partner was tethered behind me, and his voice and helmet were close to my head. "Let me turn us around so you can see." We did a little roll and spun again. "It's over there. On a day without so much haze, you'd be able to see the skyline."

I looked around. Objects below us looked like small postage stamps on a wide envelope. "Which group of building is the Jump School?" I asked.

"You see that group of building and the green field? That's where we land, but the cameraman is over there," he pointed. "Do you want to land where he is, or at the school?"

"I don't care… let's land where he is."

"Okay, hold these handles and pull when I say 'pull.' Not so hard. And remember to tuck your feet up. We may have to do a butt-landing."

By now, I was wishing we could stay up in the air for longer, but I was hungry as hell and realized there would just have to be other jumps. Not too many in my own family would believe I did this, even with the videotape and photos as evidence. I was no longer running for my life. I was flying.

[2017] Epilogue - I waited at the bus stop, pretending to be comfortable with no longer being a car owner. A black man staggered toward me mumbling about evil people in the world. He walked unsteadily, possibly the result of a night swilling drinks at a nearby gaming club. He was dressed in matching gold pinstriped jacket and pants and a black fedora. He resembled an old- time gambler from vintage movies. With strained casualness, I slid my right hand toward the small hunting knife in my jacket. I was uneasy at his closeness. His eyelids fluttered uncontrollably. His narrow face hosted two rheumy, leaking, bloodshot, blinking eyes pinched between deep facial lines. I shivered with discomfort, trying to avoid making eye contact. Instead, I inadvertently stared at the scar above the upper side of his mouth. This facial disfigurement forced his top lip to remain half-closed when he tried to smile at me. The result was a face with a half sneer. A long, thick line of spittle hung from his mouth and swung away from his face when he cocked his head to one side. His words a mix of slobbering. Maybe this man was a drug addict prone to unpredictable behaviors. I didn't want to seem anti-social, but he was clearly a person from whom I must keep my distance. So of course, he addressed me directly: "Say! Say, man. Is the hospital in that direction?"

Blinky moved closer to where I stood in the shade. He jabbed a boney finger on my forearm. "Man, my blood pressure's acting up. I tried to tell them in the restaurant, but when I entered, they grabbed me and dragged me out. I jes' told 'em I wanted to go to the *baff-room*, but this brother come running up to me. He a big black security guard, and he say, 'No! Git out!' He grab my neck, and two white guys in there *hep* him drag me out. I jes' let myself stay limp like a wet rag. Made 'em work."

"Are you telling me a brother did that to you?" I asked, surprised. "Yep. You know how some of us are"

Suddenly, Blinky shifted topic and started talking about being raised in the South. He muttered about things his grandmother had told him to never forget. Suddenly, his monologue was interrupted when a plump middle-aged white woman wearing a sports blouse, colorful form-fitting pants, and sneakers rushed up to him. Both of her arms were outstretched stiffly as she waved a few dollar bills. I eased further away to give them some space and privacy. The woman was insistent on giving Blinky the folded currency.

"Sir, here... take this! I saw what they did to you in there! We'll never go back there to eat. That was so wrong! Here! Take this. I want you to have it."

Finally, Blinky took the money and shouted his gratitude. The woman quickly retreated to a vehicle crowded with other passengers. The driver honked the car horn as they sped away. Blinky was now jubilant. "Thank you, Jesus! Thank you! God is so good!"

After this encounter, Blinky talked louder than before, and he again moved close to where I now stood. I pretended to ignore the charitable moment that had just transpired and craned my head to see the bus coming in the far distant lane of traffic. Blinking more rapidly, the man fumbled with the bills in his hand. A single dollar bill stuck between his shaking fingers as a folded twenty-dollar bill fluttered unnoticed near his feet. He jabbered on about race and good people. I pointed down to the paper currency close to his shoes. When he looked down, I walked further away from the bus stand. As my distance increased, Blinky stared at me and started shouting, "You think you're suffering me. Y'awl think that way. But I should be suffering you! I should be suffering you!"

A few moments later, standing several yards away, I peered back in the direction of the bus stand. The blinking man was now seated on the bench beneath the shade, spewing a non- stop monologue. He aimed words at two potential bus passengers who stared down at their mobile phones. Ignoring him was an effective defensive strategy. Perhaps they felt safe.

I was starting to feel jealous of the growing progression of car drivers who whizzed pass the bus stop. Within each were isolated drivers—perhaps more civilized people. They enjoyed greater personal space and were spared the noises of real living. They could choose to turn on their car radios. Yet even this encapsulation is no guarantee of personal safety. We must all make ourselves at home "suffering" from manufactured or imagined fears.

*****

The noises last night were unusual. Either intruders or would-be robbers were pressing their luck. Quietly slipping on my robe and shoes, I crept to the front door and flipped on the outside light. Before I could wrench the door open, I heard the crashing sound of metal on pavement and feet running away. I immediately noticed the two small, white, foot-high Christmas trees with colorful lights were missing from my porch. My bike was also gone. I eased past the parked cars lining the front sidewalk area. In the darkness, I saw my Walmart mountain bicycle lying in the middle of the parking lot, the rear wheel still locked and chained. The thieves had vanished. This was another close call, a warning about life in the civilized Wild West. Many people are desperate and dying. One way or another, everyone appears to be running to or away from something. Some are desperate. Others are simply crazy. More and more often, I was torn to either curse or whisper "thank you Jesus" under my breath. Our parents had done a masterful job stamping their imprint on their many siblings. I had flown high, but still wondered how much longer I would be able to hang on to my own sanity.

"A FATHER'S FRUIT"
I am my father's fruit

From the greatest tree

A legacy unfolding truths

Secrets not yet told to me.

I am my father's fruit

But who will share or need

Such strength across vast seas

A small forgotten windblown seed.

I am my father's fruit

Shadow of turbulent change

From Cross the bended back and knee

Branched scattered leaves arrange.

I am my father's fruit

Proud treasures gleam with luster sold

Legacies refined by heart so bold

Blood richer than pure gold.

I am my father's fruit.

[END]

Johannes B. Vessup, Jr., Navy Construction Battalion.

Ellene (Mom); Johannes, Jr., (Dad); Johannes, III (Brother); Jo'lene (Sister). Photographed by Aaron Vessup.

First home at 13229 Crocker Street in South Central L.A.

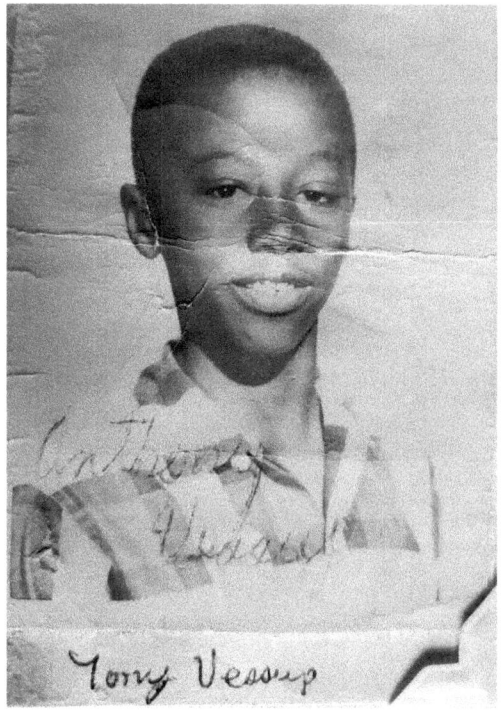

At Mark Twain Elementary School in the 6th grade 1959.

Outside Los Angeles church building, I stand in background behind dad, on right of Cousin Karen, older brother Johan on left. Dad holds Adrian and Dollie while Mark is distracted.

Christmas Greetings

Vessup family greetng card-1955

San Berdoo H.S. Senior Yearbook photo 1965

SBHS Track Team Buddies- Vessup, Lewis, Pine,
Kresge, and Lopez

JIM COSTELLO
. . . baseball, studies

AARON A. VESSUP
. . . ministerial career?

LINDA U'REN
. . . to state college

LARRY BROOKS
. . . to enter SBVC

They're Confident and Eager

S.B. Grads Tell of Hopes,

I am in local news after I give Ceremonial high school Graduation Prayer

Attendees socialize after worhship in San Bernardino Bethel Church
renovated from old Juke-Joint

My parentes, Reverend J.B. Vessup & Wife on Sunday

California State Winner for Expository Speech on ESP

AARON VESSUP   JEAN BLANCHARD

Valley Bank of America Finalists Announced

On Jan. 18 Valri Jean Blanchard and Aaron Anthony Vessup were named the two Bank of America finalists from San Bernardino Valley College. Miss Blanchard and Vessup, among 22 finalists from other colleges, will attend a luncheon at the Sheraton Hotel in Huntington Beach on Feb. 26.

From the finalists at this luncheon the top man and top woman will be chosen to compete in the state competition with the cash award of $1,000 and the title of Man and Woman of the Year going to the two winners.

students who, by balanced participation in educational, activity and community service programs, demonstrate an outstanding potential for assuming a role of leadership, and constructive citizenship.

The following criteria for the selection of candidates by each junior college and the successive event competition are the qualifications each candidate must possess.

In the field of scholarship, evidence of academic achievement

**Nominated for California Man and Woman of Year Contestants
representing San Bernardino Valley College**

ON VESSUP, a Wesleyan University junior, will Nebraska in the National Intercollegiate For st in men's oratory. Vessup won the state Men' at the association's tourney last March. The N ey will be held in May at Wayne University. Ve on is entitled "Violent Communication." He uate of SBHS and has attended SBVC and Cal State the son of Elder and Mrs. Johannes Vessup of 9

**While a Nebraska Wesleyan University senior was State
Winner in Persuasion for Violent Communication Speech**

Dating days with Vassar Jean- in San Berdoo, Calif.

AV-Vasssar with Poet Sissie Newton and daughter Kristen

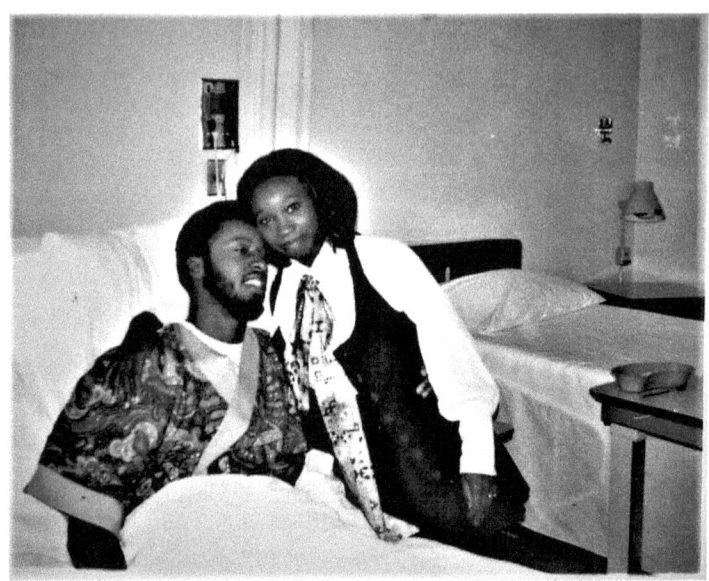

Vassar Jean provides comfort after my surgery
from baseball injury-1971

Aaron & Vassar Jean (first wife) at Illinois State Univ.
Graduate School Party

Sporting expensive hair style as Human Relations City Officer in
Bloomington, Illinois 1975

Wedding day with Pamela Rae, (second wife) at Heinz Chapel
on University of Pittsburgh campus

In Guatemala with property guardian, Santos and family.
Volcan San Pedro in background.

Meeting Muhammad Ali at graduation reception while teaching at
Texas Southern University in Houston

Producer and Host of Cultures In Focus
TV Program Episode in Northern Illinois

Interviewing the late Illinois Senator Paul Simon at Capitol
TV Studio in Washington., D.C.

**Photoman on fourth visit in Havana, Cuba in response
to invitation for group photography exhibition**

First visit to Cuba, with Ellegua Dance Drummers in Santiago

With ECC President Heath, and Literature Nobel Prize winner Derek Walcott

with Briggitte Mariana (wife #3)

Taking a time Out in Hengshui City, PRC after seminar with
Bank of China personnel

Solo Photography Exhibition on Cuba - Secret Love in Hunan,
Changsha, China

Foreign Experts receive provincial honors in Jillin, PRC

Practicing friendly Police-Community Relations in Japan

At the holy Patola in Tibet with travel guide Rainbow

At War Memorial in Belarus with curious local.

Photoman Aaron head-to-head in Cambodia

As guest in private home of Arunji Gandhi in Mumbai, India

Sharing beers with Russian Tank Unit on Siberian Express train

In Chicago Documentary Filmmaker Ken Burns gives a nod

A small Vessup family fraction meets after forty years

Family Reunion In Portland, Oregon

San Marcos a La Guna; Aaron Vessup a place for ESCAPE

www.ingramcontent.com/pod-product-compliance
Lightning Source LLC
Chambersburg PA
CBHW051512120626
46551CB00012B/891